AF443707

BUSTER KEATON'S THE GENERAL

Edited by Richard J. Anobile

Introduction by Raymond Rohauer
with special interview with
Marion Mack

A DARIEN HOUSE BOOK

UNIVERSE BOOKS
NEW YORK

A DARIEN HOUSE BOOK

© Copyright 1975 Darien House, Inc.
All rights reserved.

The frame blowups of the motion picture
THE GENERAL (1926) used by permission of and
special arrangement with Mr. Raymond Rohauer,
the exclusive representative of Buster Keaton Productions, Inc.

THE GENERAL © 1926 Joseph M. Schenck. LP 23453

THE GENERAL, Buster Keaton Film Corp., © 1954 Buster Keaton LP 16449

THE GENERAL © 1970 Jay Ward Productions, Inc. and Leopold Friedman, Trustee
LP 38511

DER GENERAL © 1961 Buster Keaton. LP 22222.

UNIVERSE BOOKS
381 Park Avenue South
New York, New York 10016

Library of Congress Catalog Card Number: 75-18998

THE FILM CLASSICS LIBRARY is the tradename
of Darien House, Inc.

All rights reserved, which includes the right to
reproduce this book or portions thereof in any form
whatsoever. The introductory article, "On the Track of
The General" by Raymond Rohauer may not be
quoted without giving both the author's name and that of
the book. For information address Darien House, Inc.
37 Riverside Drive, New York City 10023

First Printing, September 1975.

ISBN 0 87663 259 3

Printed in the United States of America

THE GENERAL, starring Buster Keaton and Marion Mack
is available in 16 and 35mm (both sound—background
and musical effects—and silent versions) for theatrical,
non-theatrical and television viewing through:
Mr. Raymond Rohauer
Representative of Buster Keaton Productions, Inc.
and Jay Ward Productions, Inc.
44 West 62nd Street, Suite 16B
New York, New York 10023

Foreword

THE GENERAL is the first silent film selected for The Film Classics Library. If this series is to be representative of a cross section of American filmmaking, several silent films must be added.

It seems that the more dialogue in a film, the easier it is to present in book form. Working on THE GENERAL bore out my suspicions in this matter. Normally I select between 1200 and 1600 frames. But for THE GENERAL I found it necessary to use over 2100 frame blowups in order to successfully retain the flow of Keaton's narrative.

This posed a number of problems, not the least of which was design. Those of you already familiar with this series will notice one major design difference in this volume; the frames stretch across two-page spreads. This facilitates the following of minute, yet important, changes of action within a given scene. And for an appreciation of Keaton this is necessary.

Following my remarks are historical and biographical comments by Raymond Rohauer and his interview with Keaton's co-star, Marion Mack. There is little to add, but a few reasons for selecting THE GENERAL.

Of all the silent film creators, Buster Keaton remains my favorite. I feel that a reassessment is in order by those who continually place Keaton behind Chaplin. As a filmmaker there can be no doubt that Keaton was Chaplin's superior. Keaton's camera is always present as an observer of human behavior; it never merely records a comic act. The grace with which Keaton directs his camera always complements the action and his players. I cannot help but feel that Keaton had an acute understanding of film. Chaplin's comedies always strike me as merely presentations of music-hall-type acts loosely held together with a minimal plot line. Chaplin does show some refinements of filmmaking technique in his later sound work. But a thorough and guilt-free comparison of their work would most assuredly establish Keaton as a more masterful filmmaker.

Keaton's comedy is also underrated. I have viewed his entire output and, of course, I've screened THE GENERAL countless times. Through all of his work one can sense the vibrations of a compassionate human as he depicts many of life's ironies.

The slam-bang comedy of Chaplin leaves much to be desired when compared to Keaton's methodical and logical buildup to humorous situations. As a total filmmaker, Keaton was able to blend his humor into a cohesive film pattern.

There is never any waiting for a Keaton funny scene as a respite from a dreary story. In all of his films, Keaton's tame comedy is an integral part of his script. Thus, he strikes a perfect cinematic balance between the two major elements in screen comedy.

Such current comic filmmakers as Woody Allen and Mel Brooks would benefit from a study of Keaton's work. Their films tend to be uneven and their audiences are literally on a roller coaster ride as they are plummeted from a peak comedy moment into a valley of doldrums. There are valid theories to support this brand of film comedy. This is exactly the technique MGM production head Irving Thalberg insisted upon when he salvaged the Marx Bros. from premature retirement in 1935. A NIGHT AT THE OPERA and A DAY AT THE RACES were constructed much like Elizabethan drama to allow the audience certain relief periods from key comedy sequences. It was also a valuable aid in prepping the audience for another funny scene. But the time and effort spent on constructing the two Marx Bros. classics just cannot be afforded today. Would Allen or Brooks dare try their film out on the road before shooting? Even if they would, could a studio sanction such expense? It is because of this that Keaton's comedy style might be more valid today. How lovely it would be to remove ourselves from our tension filled agendas and settle into a Keaton-styled comedy where the viewer continually rides the crest of a wave which insures a consistent humorous high. It would be quite a welcome relief from the rough and tumble sensationalism we are being handed.

Of all Keaton's films, THE GENERAL best displays the array of his talents. It is my hope that you will rediscover Buster Keaton's genius here and flock to revivals of his work.

Richard J. Anobile
Hollywood, California
July, 1975

On the Track of The General

by Raymond Rohauer

One of the most effective gags in THE GENERAL —visually eloquent, poignant, and funny—occurs at the end of the first reel. Buster has just tried to enlist in the Southern cause but was rejected; the recruiters didn't tell him it was because he would be more valuable to the South during the war as a railroad engineer, and so he assumes it is because of some unknown shortcoming of his. His girl, not believing the explanation, has also rejected him.

So it is a thoroughly dejected Keaton who returns to his only remaining love—"The General." When the rejection scene was being filmed, Keaton wanted a "topper"—something more than the parting of the two lovers. Always better at physical action than emotion, he devised, on the spot, a simple but effective way of showing the depth of Buster's sadness: he would sit absent-mindedly on the cross-bar of the locomotive, and will not even stir when the wheels are set in motion.

Easy to think of but not so easy to do. The engine was a museum piece; in his search for authenticity, Keaton had found a working locomotive of almost the right Civil War vintage, and had it further modified to resemble the actual "General" in every respect. There was one trouble with such an old piece of machinery, the engineer told him: it had a tendency, if the steam was not fed to it just right, to spin its wheels at the start. This would probably kill him outright, or at least very seriously injure him.

Keaton often talked about the care they took to make sure the gag didn't backfire: they tried a smooth start several times without him on the cross-bar, and when the engineer was quite sure he had the knack, Buster actually sat down and they did it again for the camera.

It has often been commented upon, in articles and books on Keaton, how imaginatively he created this "piece of business." To me, however, the real insight is in the fact that, apparently, it never occurred to Keaton how much easier—and safer—it would have been to fake it: the camera comes in a little closer so as not to show the entire engine, and meanwhile, someone out of camera range pulls the engine slowly, or perhaps pushes it in some way from behind.

Not that Keaton, or his camera crew, were unaware that such things can be done. By 1926, virtually the entire range of trick photography and gag design was well known to everyone in the movie business, and had been since the late 1890's when Georges Melies showed the magic that can be done with film. In fact, Keaton had done his share of movie trickery, as in THE PLAYHOUSE (1921), where he multiplied himself ninefold on the screen, and elsewhere. But there was such a basic honesty and simplicity in Keaton the man that using trickery where it was not absolutely necessary would not have seemed right.

To me, here is the very essence of Keaton: an unassuming directness, modesty, and total lack of ego. He never made a conscious effort to be brilliant, but simply did his best to help his screen character express himself.

Perhaps it is fortunate for all of us that Keaton never went for the higher social circles for which many of his fellow performers aspired in those days. They might have led him to intellectualize about the great social significance of his screen character or about his own genius, which made other comedians—notably Chaplin and Langdon—highly self-conscious and, eventually, spoiled them utterly for comedy. But Keaton relaxed off screen by playing baseball or cards; hence, he had to rely solely on his instinct when he was on camera, and that is how he made the great American classic, THE GENERAL.

When I met Buster Keaton—something that will always remain the highlight of my life—and was lucky enough to become both his business partner and personal friend, I asked him, as naively as others did before and many more would later, what is it that made THE GENERAL such a flawless film: Why is it that the scenes all look as if Matthew Brady was the cameraman, why there is not a single scene or gesture that's out of place, etc.

Buster couldn't tell me. First of all, he never understood why the film would continue to be considered as one of the best pieces of Americana ever to be put on the screen—it was just a comedy, a nothing . . . just to make people laugh for a couple of hours, that's all. And then he tried to suggest it may have been because they always looked for nice scenic views when devising a scene—or because the Oregon National Guard let them have so many troops—or because they went to the trouble of getting the right kinds of clothes, the train, the narrow-gauge railroad.

Of course, the secret is not in any of these things. They have been done by others, with more extras, better scenery, more historic consultants, and lots more money. But they certainly didn't make a better film; they never even approached within shouting distance of Keaton. Knowing all this, I was a little disappointed at the time; I thought he didn't want to tell me.

Only much later did I realize that if Keaton had been able to explain it to me, very likely he wouldn't have been able to make the picture in the first place. He was not educated enough to be awed by history, and so avoided the trap of pompous solemnity; and he was not sophisticated enough to be above it all, and so avoided the trap of patronizing superiority. To him, the historic event was simply an interesting experience in which an ordinary person might be expected to do extraordinary things, and that was enough.

Keaton's instinct also worked right in selecting his heroine for THE GENERAL. In Marion Mack, he found his most spirited collaborator; of all his leading ladies, she was the one who got most closely involved in the basic plot, and also one who contributed more to the success of the film by creating a perfect foil for him.

It has always been required of Keaton heroines to be slightly muddle-headed: First, because it made his superhuman exertions on their behalf seem even more comical, and second, because it would explain why they often did things that actually hindered or endangered his noble deeds, and put him into even worse troubles to get out of. (On a more abstract level, their empty-headedness also served to show what an incurable romantic the screen Keaton was: What he saw in them, clearly, was something only he could see, and this was in keeping with the surrealistic world which he created for himself. But of course, Keaton would have never been able to articulate this.)

A typical Keaton leading lady, therefore, had comparatively little to do: She had to get herself into some kind of trouble, and then wait for him to overcome impossible obstacles to get her out of it; at the fade-out, she would then fall into his arms at last—only to make the viewer wonder what he would do with her. For Keaton was obviously in his element only in the act of fighting against awesome odds to win the favors of his lady fair. Give him a balky engine to tame, rapids to swim, ocean liners to sail, motorcycles to ride, death-defying leaps to perform, and he knew just what to do. But once all the villains were vanquished and elements conquered, the girl was his: And now, faced with the reality of what up to now he obviously had only romanticized in his imagination, he appears ill at ease; his expression always at this point suggests that he is vaguely aware something is now expected of him but he is not quite sure what it may be.

Marion Mack, however, escaped this stereotype of a Keaton heroine. Since she does not just passively wait but helps to effect much of her own rescue right alongside him, there is more interaction between them than between the protagonists of any other Keaton film—not even excluding THE NAVIGATOR where Kathryn McGuire may have had more actual footage with Keaton but far less initiative.

Thus, Marion came closest to making a flesh-and-blood girl out of a Keaton leading-lady role, and the only one whom we might believe capable, at the end of the film, of actually bringing him down to earth.

It was a source of great pleasure to me to discover not only that Marion Mack was still around, but that she was, like her screen image, a very friendly, forthright, and venturesome lady who was quite willing, at 70, to be subjected once more to a dose of rough handling comparable under the circumstances to what was meted out to her in the original film. In other words, she came out of the peaceful anonymity earned through forty years of absence from public view, and faced a barrage of reporters, interviewers, cameramen and autograph seekers. She went through it all with the same game spirit that she displayed so beautifully in THE GENERAL, where she let Keaton lug her around in a gunny sack, step on her, drench her with water and rough her up.

My search for the only surviving genuine Keaton heroine took years of patience: talking to all types of film buffs, people who may have conceivably worked at the studio at the same time she did, people who may know someone who knew her, etc. Once I had the information that she was probably living under her married name, the search narrowed considerably. Fortunately, unlike many Hollywood girls, Marion only married once, and her husband, Louis Lewyn, was fairly well known around movietown, having been a producer of shorts and features for many years. And thus, finally, the search ended in 1972.

Joey Marion McCreery, alias Marion Mack, turned out to be living quietly in a small California community, a widow since Mr. Lewyn's passing in 1971. An easy person to talk to, she still possessed that aura of charm which must have made Keaton want her for his leading lady; the lively eyes, the unruly curls, and the readiness to tackle something new were all there.

The reminiscences of Buster and the making of THE GENERAL flowed fast and easy. Before long, we were discussing something I had dreamed of for years: re-tracing the route of "The General," visiting the location where the film was shot up in Oregon, and maybe even re-visiting the old engine itself in its museum in Georgia.

As it turned out, that was only the beginning. Suddenly, everybody wanted to see Keaton's leading lady; subsequently, she made personal appearances in Toronto, Tokyo, London and New York, reminisced on several television talk shows, and got write-ups in a number of newspapers. In Oregon, she met an electrician and a couple of extras who worked on THE GENERAL with her, 47 years earlier; in Georgia, she posed with the engine on whose replica she had spent so many happy hours with Keaton; and everywhere, she dispensed autographs to fans who had not even been born when she was giving what proved to be her last screen performance with the immortal Keaton.

A great personal triumph for the plucky little lady from California, and a source of immense gratification to a veteran film fan and collector from Buffalo . . . and none of it would have been possible if, a century before, a daring soldier in Chattanooga had not dreamed up one of the most bizarre plots of the Civil War, and if, a half-century later, the plot had not inspired a Kansas-born comedian to fashion an artistic masterpiece of the cinema.

The real-life drama that started this whole chain of events had nothing comical about it, but it certainly had some unusual elements. It was without a doubt the first occasion when trains, at that time just about 30 years in operation in this country, were used in a war. The time was April, 1862; the Civil War was in full sway at the end of its first year. The Northern Army stood at Chattanooga; the Southern capital and headquarters, Atlanta, was only a hundred miles from there.

In those days of poor communications, the Southern Army defending the approaches to Atlanta relied for much of its supplies on a most tenuous lifeline: the single-track, narrow-gauge railroad running roughly northwest from Atlanta. A Union spy, James J. Andrews, conceived a plan to disrupt this supply line: starting from Tennessee, his group of men would penetrate through the lines, disguised as Southerners, and steal a train somewhere near Atlanta. They would then drive it rapidly northward to Chattanooga, blowing up bridges, cutting telegraph lines, and making the track unusable to the South. The idea was that the element of surprise would give the spies enough time to accomplish this mission before an effective pursuit could be organized.

The mission went off without a hitch—up to a point. The Andrews group got into Georgia all right, and at Big Shanty, a whistlestop near Marietta, they seized a train while its passengers were being served breakfast in the station. Uncoupling the passenger cars, the spies used the locomotive and the baggage cars alone to make their way northward, stopping occasionally to plant explosives and tear down utility poles.

As it happened, though, at several points along the route there were locomotives available for shunting cars, and the Southerners were able to mount a pursuit using these engines. Only about 20 miles short of their goal of Chattanooga, the Northerners were forced to abandon their train, and were quickly rounded up; some were executed and others went to prison.

The unusually daring nature of this exploit, which became known through a written account by one of the surviving participants, William Pittenger, was obviously fine stuff for a film, with bold action, real-life drama, the thrill of a pursuit all ready for the using. But only a cinema genius like Keaton would conceive of making it as a comedy, without losing or in any way belittling the gravity of the situation.

He accomplished this by the simple expedient of focusing the story on the Southern engineer whose train was stolen, and whose indignation over this unlawful snatch was so great that the issue of the war becomes relatively secondary. In the screen Keaton, he had an ideal hero for this role: first of all, he always tackled everything in dead earnest, whether it be tying a shoelace or winning a war single-handedly. Secondly, this very earnestness made it easy for the audience to believe that such a man would feel the loss of a locomotive as personally as the loss of his girl. In fact, Keaton made sure that the point is established early in the film: he gives Marion Mack a picture of himself in which the engine occupies a very prominent position.

Thus, with a minimum of legerdemain, Keaton successfully reduced a big national conflict into a personal one, and established a believable hero with comical possibilities.

Next, he eliminated all the real-life details which would have needlessly complicated the film, such as the fact that several engines, instead of one, were used in the actual chase. Finally, while remaining true to the spirit of history, he tied up the loose ends of the story into a satisfying dramatic resolution; thus, the return pursuit back to the Southern lines as well as the whole love interest are Keaton's embellishments.

To film his epic, Keaton wanted to stay as close to authenticity as possible; undoubtedly, he would have filmed the whole thing in Georgia if the railroad had still existed. Unfortunately, the original narrow-gauge line between Chattanooga and Atlanta had long since been replaced by a double-track, standard-gauge link which did not even follow the route of the Civil War line, and was far too straight and modern-looking to serve his purpose.

He did find the original stolen engine, "The General"—which the North apparently annexed, after all, as in 1926 it was reposing, forgotten, in a Chattanooga depot. This made it comparatively easy to find another engine of similar vintage and wheel configuration when a suitable narrow-gauge railroad winding through unspoiled scenery was at last unearthed in Oregon, and to make a few alterations on the engine so that in the end it did look exactly like the genuine "General." Similar alterations were made on the pursuit engine, "The Texas," which was also preserved and on display in Atlanta.

The filming took place during the summer of 1926 on a rugged, picturesque stretch of a lumber company's trackage near Culp Creek, about 20 miles east of Cottage Grove, Oregon. On the Row River nearby, the film company built a wooden bridge with tracks, so that one of the engines, "The Texas," could be spectacularly wrecked in one of the most memorable scenes of the picture. (It was a tourist attraction in the river for years thereafter, until the salvage drive of World War II caused removal of most of the usable metal, and a private company removed the rest some years later.)

For the record, THE GENERAL was first screened publicly in Tokyo, Japan, on December 31, 1926. Its London premiere was held January 17, 1927 and its New York opening February 6, 1927.

I will not belabor the obvious by describing the film's enduring fame and success. Perhaps it would suffice to say that in my travels around the world, I have yet to find a country where THE GENERAL was not shown, or is not instantly identified as one of the greatest pictures of all time; and there probably is not a basic film course taught anywhere without THE GENERAL as one of the required viewing assignments.

As if to prove Keaton's thesis about the comic possibilities in this subject, "The General" stole the spotlight once again in the late 1960's—as a result, fittingly, of another conflict between the North and the South. The engine suddenly appeared on view in Atlanta; it was now Chattanooga's turn to claim that it was stolen, and nothing less but a court wrangle straight out of Gilbert and Sullivan would do to resolve the issue.

As of this writing, "The General" is on display at Kennesaw, Georgia, near Marietta—which seems appropriate enough, since not only was this one of the mainway stations of the crucial railroad, but also a genuine Civil War battleground. From a practical viewpoint, it adds a point of interest for visitors to Kennesaw Mountain National Battlefield Park.

However, one never knows about those treacherous Yankee raiders, and so a full-time marshall is on duty to keep all hands off the throttle of "The General."

As to Keaton's "General," it was returned to the lumber company after use in the film, and remained on duty until it wore out and was scrapped.

Raymond Rohauer:
Well, Marion, how do you feel now that you've heard the people out there?

Marion Mack:
I still can't believe it. They treated me as if I was Gloria Swanson. I'm really glad now that you found me and brought me out here, although to tell you the truth, at first I thought you were some kind of nut. But only for a little while!

RR: I'm glad we did it, too. But I must say you were one of the most elusive ladies I ever had to pursue.

MM: You know, I still wonder how you actually tracked me down. I wasn't listed anywhere, and practically nobody had my address.

RR: Yes, I know, I tried everything: *Variety*, the Screen Actors Guild, the Academy of Motion Picture Arts and Sciences—nothing! At MGM, they only knew that up to 1940, your husband was pro-

ducing shorts for them. This made me realize you might be traceable under your husband's name, but what threw me there is that I was looking for Marion, and you were using your real first name, Joey.

MM: Yes, I thought that would be safe enough. And it was, for all these years. You know when you finally got me on the phone and asked me if I was Marion Mack, I was so shocked I couldn't answer you for a while. And when I'm at a loss for words, that's something!

RR: Do you know how I finally got to you? I just simply looked up the name Lewyn in the Los Angeles phone book. Of course, there was neither Marion nor Louis listed, but there was another Lewyn, and I called up and they said they didn't know themselves, but that a member of their family who happened to be living in Switzerland was a

distant relative of yours. So, as I was just then on my way to France to attend the Avignon film festival, I contacted the lady in Switzerland while I was there, and once she said you lived in Costa Mesa I called you up at once.

MM: Yes, that was part of what threw me. All these years no one knew about me, and then you call me from Paris and right off the bat say: "Are you Marion Mack?" I thought someone was playing a practical joke on me again, as Buster used to do.

RR: Marion, I wonder if you would mind going over some of the things you were just talking about with your fans out there, so that we could get it on the record, so to speak. By the way, is this the first time you made a personal appearance with the film?

MM: Oh yes, it is. You know back in 1927 neither Buster nor the producers thought much of the picture. It was a routine comedy, and they didn't make any big fuss about opening it, no personal appearances or anything. And also, by that time I had other interests, and in fact I was practically out of the picture business when the film opened — at least out of the acting stage of the business. So tonight is my very first personal promotion with the film. In fact, this is the first time I ever saw THE GENERAL and didn't have to pay!

RR: You mean you had to buy a ticket to see your own performance?

MM: And not just once, either. My husband and I attended the opening of the picture, but purely as spectators. We both liked it, of course, but we were surprised when it took off as it did. It was the audiences that made it such a hit, the studio never realized what a gem they had on their hands until the money started rolling in. And in later years, every once in a while I used to go to one of the revival theaters when THE GENERAL was showing. At first I used to tell them I was the co-star, but I think they either didn't believe me, or it meant nothing to them. I was

sort of hoping one of the managers would let me in free, but they used to say something like "Oh, really?" or "That's nice," and then they would politely show me where the box office was. You see what fun it is to be a famous movie star!

RR: Don't give it a second thought, Marion. Back in the early fifties, when I ran a theater in Los Angeles, Buster Keaton himself used to come and buy a ticket like anyone else, because none of my ticket takers recognized him. Anyway, Marion, could we have a little of your background —such as, how did you ever come to Hollywood in the first place?

MM: Well, Raymond, believe it or not, I just wrote a letter to Mack Sennett, and that's all there was to it. I was just a high school girl from Mammoth, Utah, and I said I wanted to be in the movies and enclosed a few snapshots, and they were real polite and Sennett's manager wrote back they would be happy to interview me if I ever came to Hollywood. It sounds like fiction but it's true. You see, this was in 1920 and it could still happen like this.

RR: Did they just say you should

come right out to Hollywood?

MM: Not just like that, I had to be properly chaperoned. Now it so happened my father was married for the second time, and my step-mother was only about 24, and I was 18. So she agreed to help me, and we went to Hollywood.

RR: So you went in and just got a job at the first studio you contacted?

MM: Would you believe it, Raymond, that I got not one but two offers? You see, at about the same time, there was a beauty contest at the Ince Studio, and so I entered it, too. That is, I sent in my picture and that was it. They would let me know, one of those things. So naturally, I thought nothing more of it, and went over to Sennett's Studio and saw Jack Waldron, that was Sennett's manager, and I got hired at $25 a week. And then about a week later, there was my picture in the paper that I won the contest at Ince's. Now they wanted me, and I told them I was already working for Sennett, and Ince's publicity man got a little mad at me. Hans Sternberg, I think his name was.

RR: So how did you finally solve the problem?

MM: Well, I didn't want to work for Ince because I already had a job with Sennett, and in those days Sennett was the king. But Sternberg insisted that I must at least pose for some Ince publicity, at the Billion Dollar Theater I believe, and so I thought that's the least I could do. And the funny thing is, when those publicity pictures got back to Sternberg, he showed them to Louis Lewyn, who later became my husband, and Lou said: "What a lemon! How did you ever pick her?"

RR: Oh, really? Then how did you and Mr. Lewyn get together?

MM: Well, some time later Lou came over to the Sennett lot to take some publicity pictures of some of the girls. And all of a sudden he saw me, and either I looked better in make-up or those Ince photos must have been really bad, because now he didn't recognize me as a lemon but actually asked me to pose for some pictures for him separately from the other girls. And after the posing, he kept asking me if he could bring me home. I told him my father wouldn't let me date, but he insisted and so I let him take me to my house and on the way he asked how I got in the

movies. So I said: "There was this contest at the Ince Studio and I won it," and he nearly fainted. And then I learned the whole story of what he thought of me at first, but I finally married him, anyway, and it worked out fine.

RR: That's quite a story, Marion. But tell me, what did you think of Mack Sennett?

MM: I was a little scared of him at first. He sounded a little rough, you know. But in those days I looked a little like Mabel Normand, who was Sennett's sweetheart, so I guess he liked me.

RR: How did you get your screen name? Did Sennett give it to you?

MM: No. At Sennett's, they called me Joanne McGuire. Later, when I went to work for the Little Mermaid and Sunshine Comedies, they wanted me to take another name, so I just took the middle part of my real name. I was born Joey Marion McCreery, so I clipped off Joey on one side and Creery on the other, and what was left was Marion Mc. All I had to do was spell out the "Mc." Marion Mack.

RR: All right, you say you left Sennett. Why was that?

MM: Well, I wanted to do a little more

than just stand around in a bathing suit, so I took the first good offer that came along. By about 1922 I was making feature films, and then in 1923 Lou and I were married, and as you know he became later quite a big producer, and right from the start he let me write some of the scripts for the films he was doing, and I liked that. In this way, I made MARY OF THE MOVIES with my husband in 1923, and then THE CARNIVAL GIRL in 1926.

RR: Now tell me, Marion, how did you get to work with Keaton on his most important film?

MM: Buster was looking for an old-fashioned girl, with long curly hair, for the character of Annabelle Lee, because they wanted everything to look just right for the Civil War period. Well, Percy Westmore, who was making up Norma Talmadge for some picture, heard this from her, and of course she knew it because her sister, Natalie, was married to Keaton. And Percy mentioned that he knew a girl with just the right hair, because he had been my make-up man on CARNIVAL GIRL. And Norma said to Percy he should try to find out if I was available, and he called me and first thing he said was: "I hope you still have those long curls you had in CARNIVAL GIRL!" Well, Raymond, this was the year everyone was bobbing their hair, and so only about a couple of days before I cut my hair short, too, and I told it to Percy and he said, "Don't worry, we'll give you a fall or something."

RR: A what?

MM: A fall, you know, a wig. So that's what I wore to the interview with Buster Keaton.

RR: Who was present there? Was Keaton personally in on the interview?

MM: Yes, he was there, but he didn't say much. The guys who really talked to me were Lou Anger, the studio manager, and Clyde Bruckman. And then they sort of looked at Buster, and Buster said he thought I would do, and so I was hired right then and there.

RR: Up to this time, had you ever met Keaton?

MM: No, this was the first time. But, of course, everybody in town knew about him, he was well known, but he didn't get around to many of the smart parties and places, and stuck pretty much to his own pals.

RR: Now, let's take up the story of THE GENERAL. How long did it take to shoot the picture?

MM: We were six months on it. Actually, we went up to Oregon twice. First in the spring, around April, we stayed for about four months. Then we went back to Hollywood in September to do the studio scenes, and in October we went back to Cottage Grove for some more outdoor shooting.

RR: How was it set up on location?

MM: We all stayed at the Cottage Grove Hotel, and every morning we took that little train which you can see in the picture, and we rode out to location. It took about an hour. Buster had his own chef with him, Willy his name was, and he prepared hot lunch on location so that we could stay there all day.

RR: How did they shoot the picture? Was there a script?

MM: They used what I think today would be called just an outline. Not a real script as we now know it. I mean, they told you what the scene was, but you were expected to make up your own bits of business, and if anybody had an idea they would try it and see how it played. Like when I have the scene where I'm getting on the train Buster is driving, and I'm still supposed to be mad at him for not enlisting, I made a big business out of admiring the medal my brother was wearing, and polishing his uniform buttons, just to show how much I admired him, because of course I know that Buster is looking at me. And this was not in any script, but they said it looked cute and so it stayed in.

RR: Can you think of other incidents like that where you improvised right on camera?

MM: Oh yes, we did that all the time. You know the scene on the engine where I'm supposed to feed the fire, I'm supposed to be a little dumb about it. So somebody said I should get hold of a log with a knothole in it, and throw it away. I did that, but I didn't think the audience would understand it, and then I saw a very small piece of wood, and I picked it up and threw it in. Buster liked it, so right away he built it up; I mean he picked up an even smaller piece, just a splinter really, to see if I would be dumb enough to use that, too. And of course I did, and so he jumped on me as if he was going to choke me, but at the last moment he really gave me a little peck on the cheek. I think I got that kiss more for thinking

14

of the gag than for anything else. And none of this was in written form at all.

RR: Did you get to know Keaton very well as a person?

MM: Buster was really a shy person. Some people said he was aloof, but his aloofness was mostly just shyness, I think. He wasn't easy to know very closely. Off screen, he always had his friends to play baseball with; why, sometimes they stopped the train when they saw a place to play baseball, and everything would be delayed by a couple of hours. And also, he had Natalie with him there, so there wasn't much socializing, actually. I had never worked with a leading man like that before, I can tell you, usually they were outgoing and chummy, but Buster just stuck to the job and to his little clique, and that was all. At first I felt a little bit, I'd say, ignored or slighted, but then he got a bit more friendly as he lost some of his shyness, and he turned out to be a very nice and warm person. And a very humble one, too, that's the surprising part.

RR: When did you feel that the ice was broken?

MM: I guess when he started playing jokes on me. In his book, when he made you the butt of some practical joke, that meant you were OK. Funny you should mention breaking ice, one of the first gags he ever played on me was to have a couple of the guys grab me from behind and hang me upside down over a cake of ice as we were on the way to location on the train. I already had my make-up on, which took about an hour to do, and all of it got ruined and I was very uncomfortable, so as soon as they put me down again I went and punched Buster in the eye. It gave him such a shiner they had to stop shooting for a week. This was before I understood that he meant no harm. He'd go to any length to get a laugh, but there was no malice in his practical jokes.

RR: So he kept it up even after you hit him in the eye?

MM: Oh boy, he sure did. Like the time he found out that sometimes I used to like to take my bike and go up about three miles from Cottage Grove to a spot on the river that was nice and secluded, and there I would swim. So he and a couple of his buddies sneaked up after me one day, and found where I left my clothes and tied them up in such knots that I couldn't unravel them. And so I had to pedal back to Cottage Grove in my bathing suit, and this was quite a shocking thing to do in 1926, you simply didn't ride a bike in your bathing suit in those days, and a wet one at that!

RR: Did Buster play any tricks on you in front of the camera?

MM: Yes, he did. You know, I was told at the beginning that there would be a double to do all the stunts, and a girl was actually hired and was standing by, so I was satisfied. But then, as Buster got to know me better I guess he decided I was a good sport, and would you believe it, they never used that girl once as far as I know. Like in the scene where I'm in the sack and Buster is supposed to step all over me. He told me to get in the sack, and then they would cut and let the other girl replace me for the rough stuff. But next thing I knew, he was stepping all over me, and the cameras were grinding. But I didn't get mad at him that time, I must say he knew just how to do it so it wouldn't hurt me. I guess it was his vaudeville training.

RR: Is that you in the scene on top of the box car where you are drenched from the water tank?

MM: That was another time when Buster said all I had to do was help set up the scene, and then they would cut and the extra would get the soaking. Now, as soon as we're up there Buster grabs the big spout and it comes off accidentally the wrong way, and we get all wet. Right away, Buster realized it was probably funny, and so now he puts the spout in the right way but also pulls the wire that releases the water, and I got soaked the second time. So I got it twice, and both times I didn't know it was coming, so the surprise you see on my face up there is for real. Boy, I sure was as wet as a drowned rat that time. But it would never have looked so good if it hadn't really happened by accident the first time, and if Buster hadn't helped a little the second time. He had all his crew trained to keep the cameras running even if something unexpected happened, you never knew what was going to turn out good when you saw it on the screen.

RR: Do you remember the scene where you're climbing through a small opening in one of the cars? Was it really as hard as it looked?

MM: Buster wanted it to look as if we were having a hard time, so I

had to put out one leg first and pretend I couldn't quite make it, and then try it the other way. Actually, with those long skirts it was a bit awkward, and also the train was actually moving, so there was some danger. I'm sure they would never do it today with the real stars, they'd have stunt men or they'd fake the train motion in some way by back projection. But in those days we never gave it a second thought, we just did it.

RR: When you get into the sack the first time, there in the woods when Buster is supposed to pick you up, was that really you in there when he lifts it?

MM: Yes, again, like I told you, he was supposed to let the other girl get in, she was about ten pounds lighter, anyway, and so I didn't think Buster would be too anxious to lug me around. But, as I told you, by now I think he got used to me, and so he always found a way to keep me in the scene. But you know, in this scene another accident happened which they left in; he is supposed to empty the sack which is full of Army boots, and when he did it his own shoes came off and for a while he couldn't find the right ones among all the other shoes. It was never planned

but since it looked funny, they kept it in the picture. And then he gets me in the sack and all of a sudden I feel he's picking me up, but he was stronger than I thought, and it never fazed him a bit. And that's really my hand you see uncoupling the wagons from inside the sack later.

RR: Which scenes were done in the studio in Hollywood?

MM: Very few, really. The one that gave us the most trouble was the night scene when Buster and I are running away from the cottage. We were three weeks doing that, and even here in the studio he wanted to do it as true to life as possible, and so we did it on the back lot at night, with rain and wind machines. We came in every night at about 7, and stayed until maybe one a.m., and this went on for three weeks, and each night we got soaked to the skin, it's a wonder we didn't catch pneumonia. But as I said, we just never thought much about it. It had to be done, so we did it.

RR: What other scenes did you do in Hollywood?

MM: The indoor scenes, but as you know there were only a few. Some of the supposed indoor scenes, like the one with Buster in the recruiting office, these were actually done in Cottage Grove outdoors, with fake walls but no ceiling. Also the scene at the beginning, where Buster comes to call on me and I sort of play a trick on him and follow him to my house, that was all done up on location.

RR: How many times did you usually run through a scene?

MM: Most of them Buster okayed after one or two takes. The only ones that had to be timed to precision were the gags, and they sometimes took five or six tries. But they also shot quite a few whole scenes which were never used in the finished picture, because Buster was a perfectionist and he only used the best scenes. That's why the whole film is so tightly edited, he took out all the scenes which would have dragged it out.

RR: Well, now, I hope you don't mind telling us, Marion, why is it that you never made another picture after THE GENERAL. Surely, with the film being such an enormous success, you could have had your pick of directors and films?

MM: Well, Raymond, I was really an old-fashioned girl at heart. And when Lou told me he didn't like me to be away on location so long, I realized we would always have friction if I stayed in the business. Besides, he needed me to help him write the short films he was now producing for Paramount, and I truly enjoyed that side of it even more than I liked acting. Since my marriage meant more to me than anything else, I just refused all offers, and finally they stopped asking me. And you see, it worked, Lou and I stayed married even when everyone in Hollywood was always getting divorced, and we were only about two years away from our golden anniversary when he passed away.

RR: Did you see Keaton anymore after the filming?

MM: Yes, we remained friends and saw him off and on. I remember one time, right after we finished THE GENERAL, we were invited to a New Year's Eve party in Caliente, at a night club owned by Joe Schenck, and Buster was there, and he did one of his famous slides. As I told you, he would go anywhere for a laugh, and he did one of the bits he learned on stage, slid on his stomach right across the whole dance floor. And the reason he did it, he saw Peggy Joyce, she was one of the supposed glamor girls with more jewelry than anyone in the world, sitting there across the floor, so he did the slide and pretended to get all mixed up and accidentally on purpose he tipped over her chair and spilled her all over the floor. I guess he just wanted to take her down a peg.

RR: There was a lot of publicity about Buster's drinking problem. Did you ever witness any excessive drinking?

MM: No, that all came later. He certainly never drank while working, at least not so that it would affect him, or I'm sure I would have noticed. This was still when he was in top form. Later, his marriage went on the rocks, and they wouldn't let him make films the way he wanted to make them, and I felt really sorry for him. That's what I think drove him to drink. But by then we had drifted apart, anyway, and we saw him very seldom. I prefer to remember him when he was at his best, when we were playing little jokes on each other up in Cottage Grove on our little train. That was the real Buster: Funny as hell on the screen and a true friend off the screen. They just don't make them like that anymore.

RR: They never did even then, Marion. He was unique.

MM: You said it, Raymond. He was the best of them all.

Acknowledgments

I would like to take this opportunity to thank those individuals whose cooperation has made this book possible. Rights to produce this book were granted to us by Mr. Raymond Rohauer. Raymond is a dedicated film historian and collector who, more than any other individual or organization, has preserved the work of Buster Keaton. Special thanks also go to Mrs. Buster (Eleanor) Keaton.

Once again Alyne Model, Jan Kohn and George Norris of Riverside Film Associates in New York have carefully transferred my marks from print to negative and assured that the frames I selected were the frames to be blown up.

The blowups were produced at Vita Print in New York where Saul Jaffe saw to it that all precautions were taken for production of the best possible image.

Our designer, Harry Chester Associates, ingeniously laid out this book with an eye towards retaining the flavor of Keaton's style. Fitting over 2100 frames into this format was quite a challenge which Mr. Chester's group successfully met.

And Helen Garfinkle at Darien House who, now that I am in California, does a grand job of keeping all my projects in coordination.

—Richard J. Anobile.

NOTE TO THE READER

You will notice a fuzziness or graininess in some photos. This is due to the fact that *every* photo is a blow-up of the individual frames of the film itself. All possible means have been taken to insure clarity but inconsistencies in negative quality of this 40-year-old film account for the variations of photo densities you will observe. These frames, in addition to their age and fragile state, were, of course, meant to be seen at rapid speed on a screen; by arresting the action at a single frame, we have, necessarily and artificially, frozen that scene to better view it in book form. But at the same time we have also exposed all the dirt, grains and imperfections which the theatre viewer would not normally see. However, only in this manner, by going directly to the film rather than using publicity shots or stills, could the authenticity of the scenes be preserved.

Also, in keeping as true to the film as possible, lap dissolves and fades were left in where necessary. The effect of a lap dissolve to the reader will be the appearance of two seemingly superimposed photos. The purpose here, as it was the director's, is to bridge the time and place gap between two scenes.

Joseph M. Schenck

PRESENTS

BUSTER KEATON

IN

"THE GENERAL"

A UNITED ARTISTS PRODUCTION

Written and Directed
by
Buster Keaton
and
Clyde Bruckman

Adapted by
Al Boasberg and Charles Smith

Photographed by
Dev Jennings and Bert Haines

Technical Director   Lighting Effects
Fred Gabourie   Denver Harmon

THE CAST

Annabelle Lee..............Marion Mack
Captain Anderson........Glen Cavender
General Thatcher..............Jim Farley
A Southern General....Frederick Vroom
Her father...................Charles Smith
Her brother..............Frank Barnes
Three Union Generals.......{ Joe Keaton
                             Mike Donlin
                             Tom Nawn
Johnnie Gray.............Buster Keaton

The Western and Atlantic
Flyer speeding into
Marietta, Ga., in the Spring
of 1861.

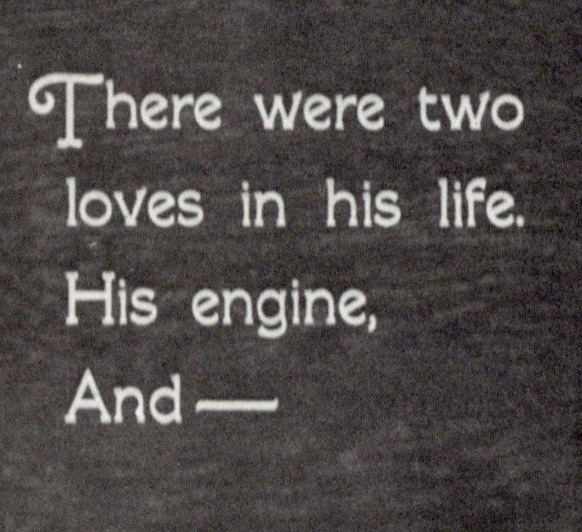
There were two
loves in his life.
His engine,
And—

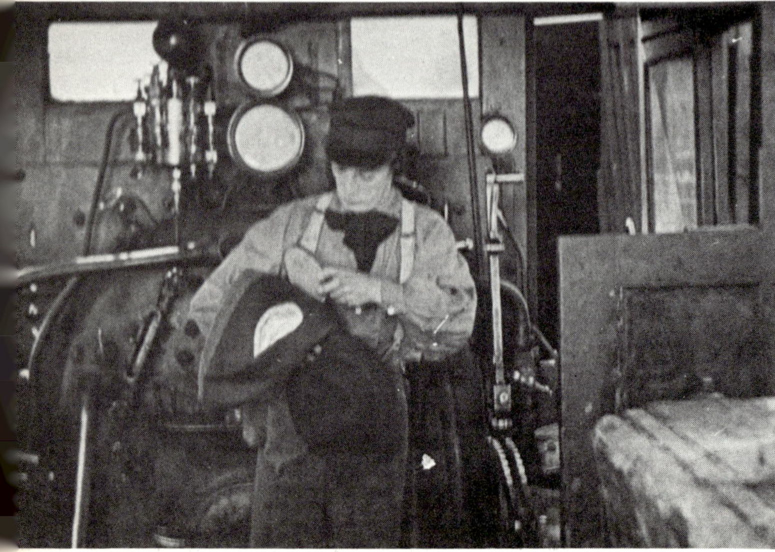

'Fort Sumter' has been
fired upon.'

'Then the war is here.'

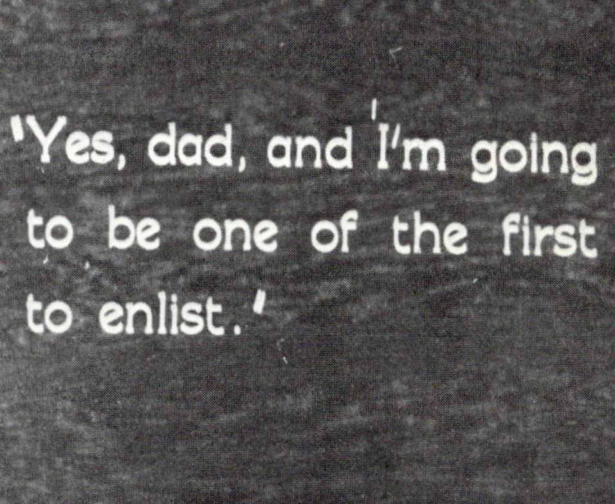

'Yes, dad, and I'm going to be one of the first to enlist.'

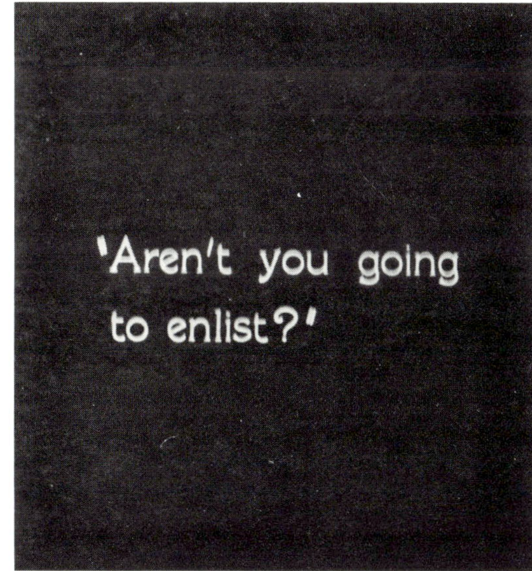
'Aren't you going
to enlist?'

RECRUITING OFFICE
SOUTHERN
COTTON GROWERS
EXCHANGE

'Occupation?'

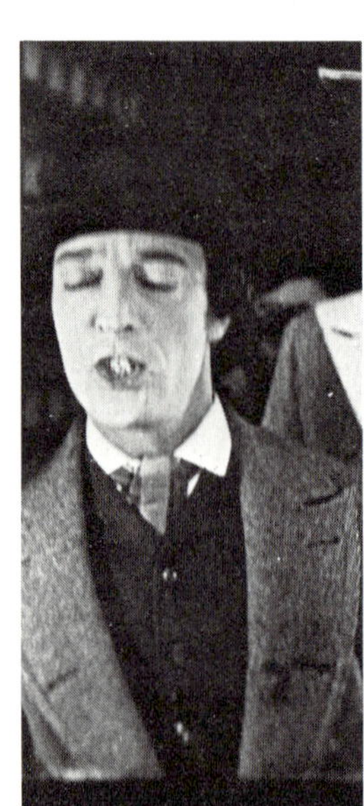

'Engineer on the Weste.
and Atlantic Railroad.'

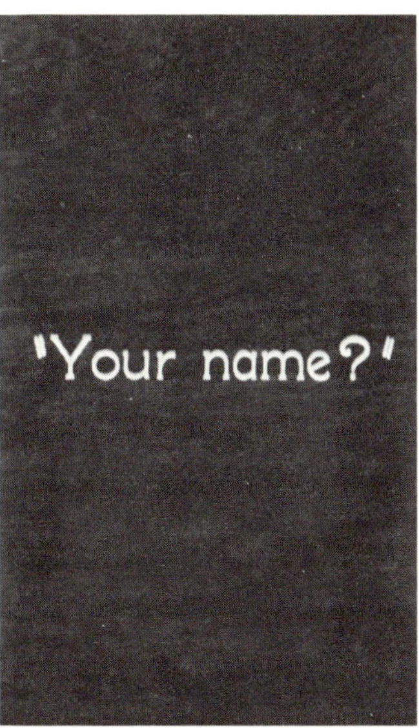
'Your name?'

'Johnnie Gray.'

'Don't enlist him. He is
more valuable to the
South as an engineer.'

"We can't use you."

  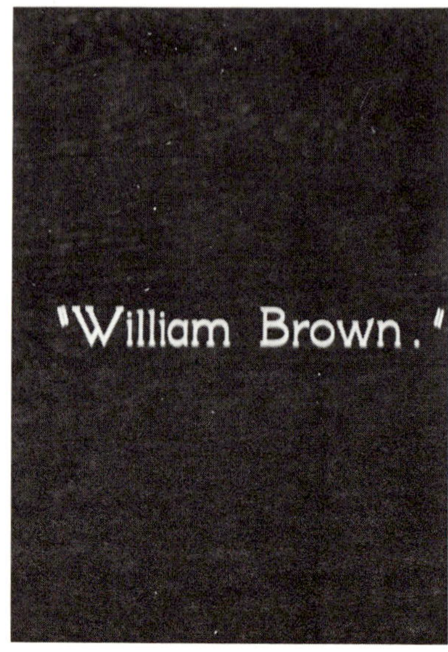

"William Brown."

Occupation?"

"Bartender."

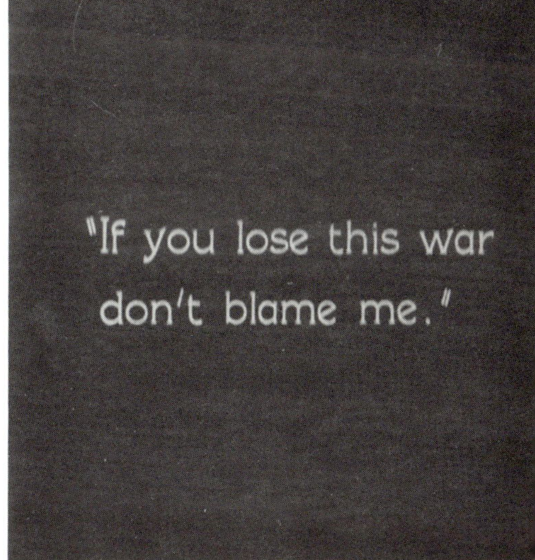
"If you lose this war
don't blame me."

  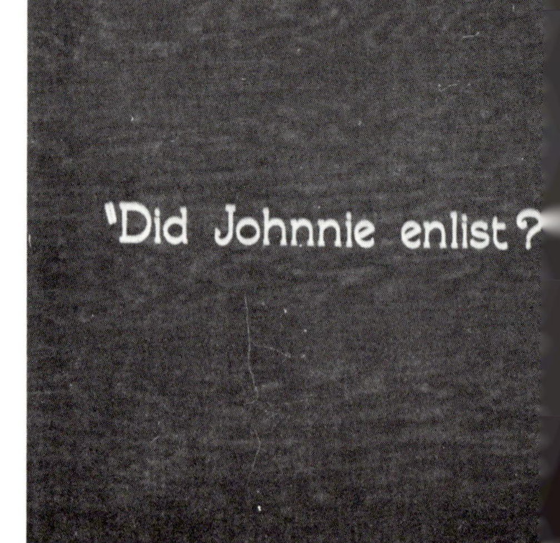
'Did Johnnie enlist?

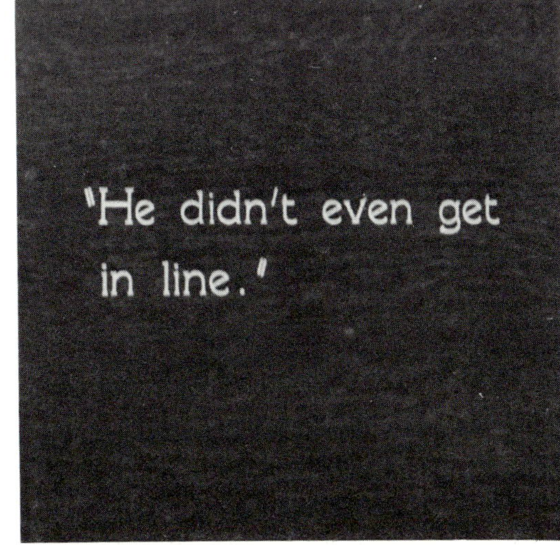
'He didn't even get
in line.'

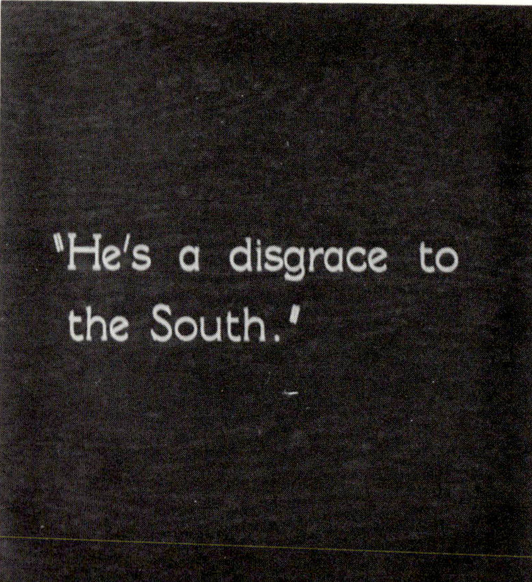
"He's a disgrace to
the South."

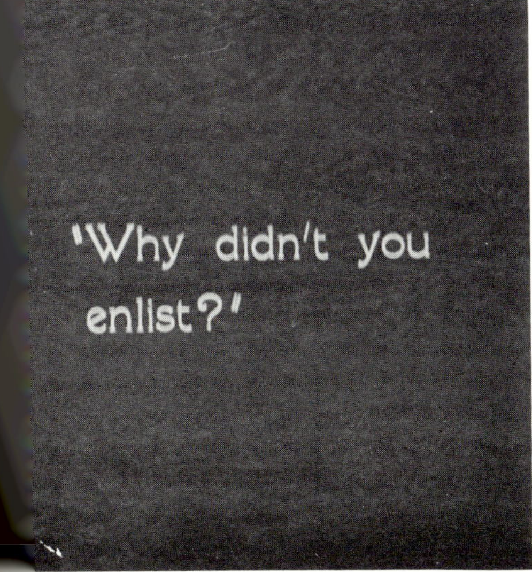
'Why didn't you enlist?'

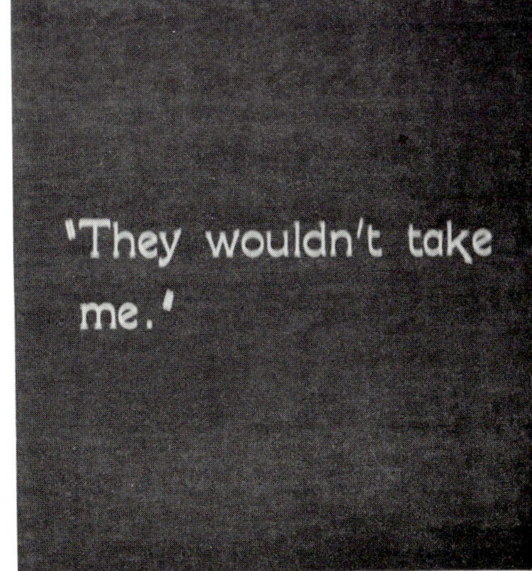
'They wouldn't take me.'

"Please don't lie — I
don't want you to
speak to me again
until you are in
uniform."

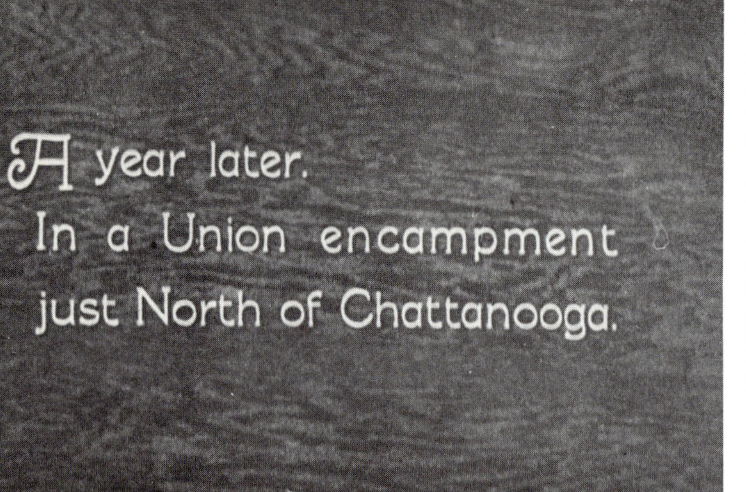
A year later.
In a Union encampment
just North of Chattanooga.

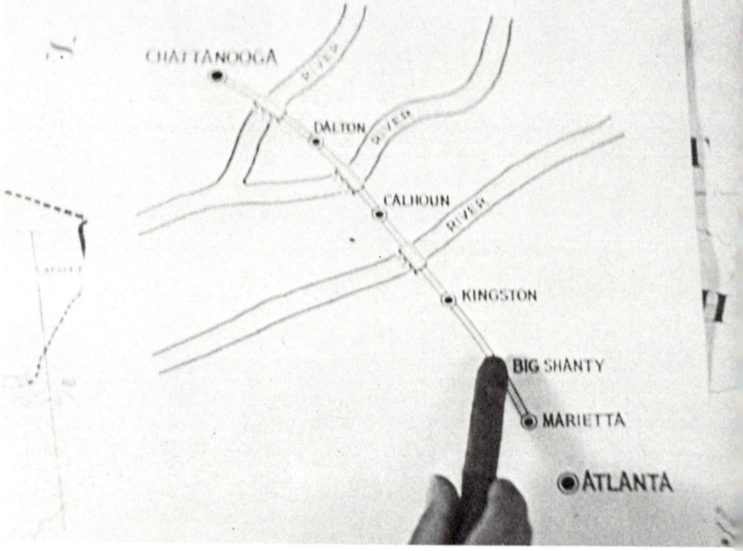
CHATTANOOGA
DALTON
CALHOUN
KINGSTON
BIG SHANTY
MARIETTA
ATLANTA

'We will enter the South
as civilians coming from
the neutral state of
Kentucky to join the
Southern cause.'

'Then the day you steal
the train I will have
General Parker advance
to meet you.'

General Thatcher, and
his chief spy, Captain
Anderson.

'I know every foot of this
railroad from Marietta to
Chattanooga — and with
ten picked men I cannot
fail.'

At Big Shanty we will steal
the train while the passengers
and crew are at dinner, and
proceeding North we will burn
every bridge, cutting off the
supplies of the army now
facing you.'

MARIETTA

W&A.R.R.

16

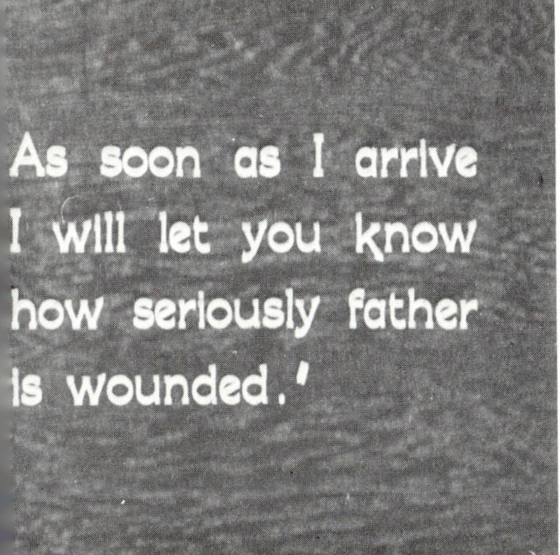
As soon as I arrive
I will let you know
how seriously father
is wounded.'

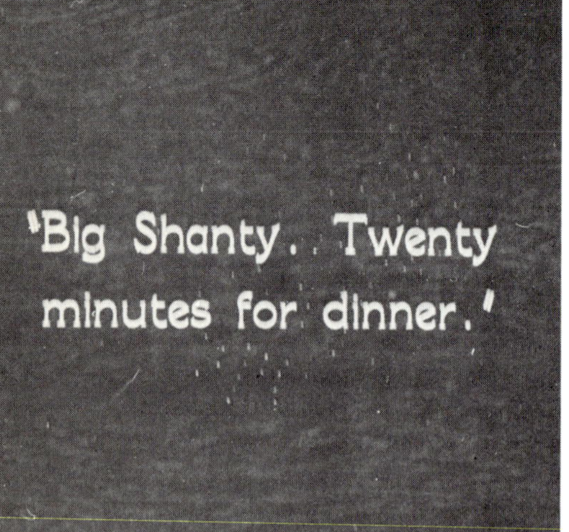
'Big Shanty. Twenty
minutes for dinner.'

W.B.&R.R.

W.B.&R.R.

W.B.&R.R.

B.A.R.R.

W.&A.R.R.

W.&A.R.R.

R.R.
W.&A.R.R.

R.R.
18
W.&A.R.R.

W.&A.R.R.

W. & A.

  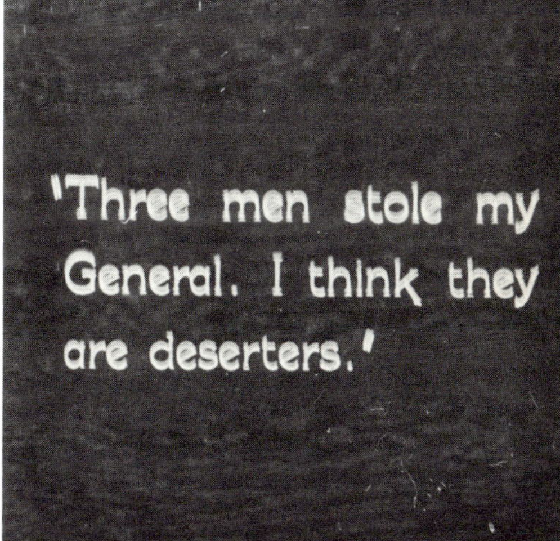
'Three men stole my
General. I think they
are deserters.'

W.8.A.R.R.

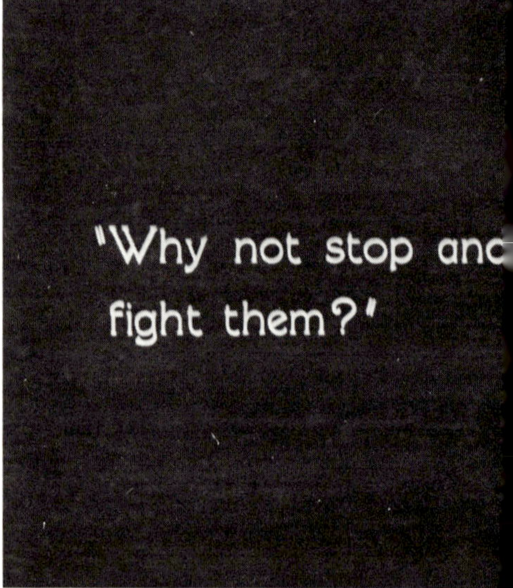
"Why not stop and
fight them?"

W.&A.R.

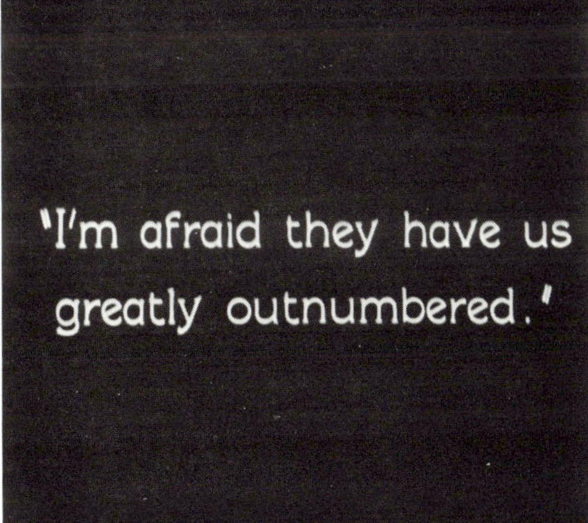
'I'm afraid they have us
greatly outnumbered.'

R.R.

R.R.

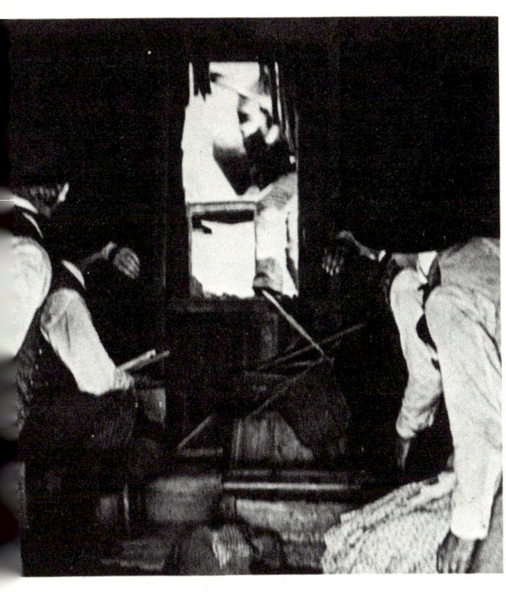
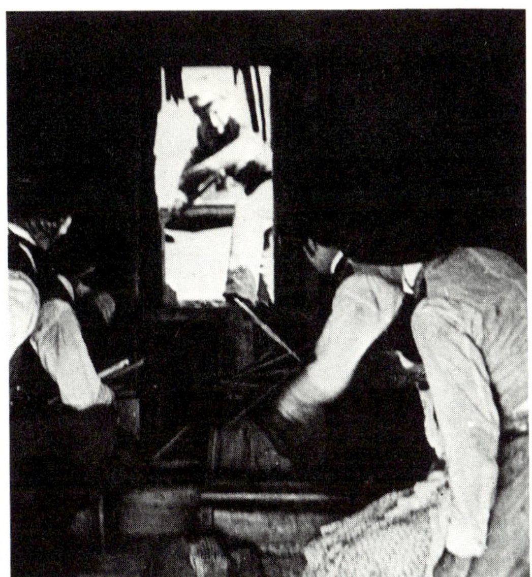

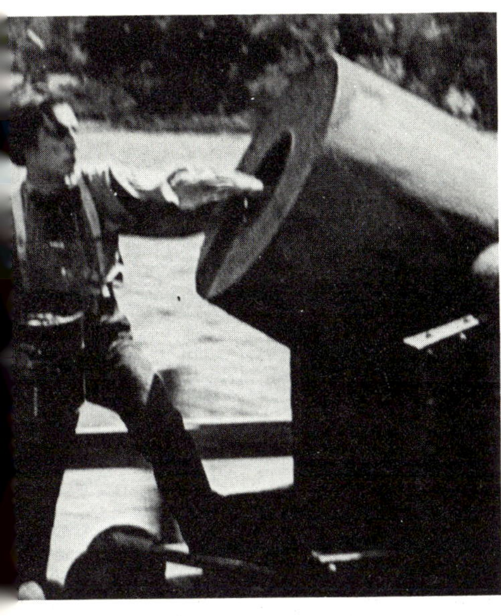

W.&.A.R.R.
W.&.A.R.R.

W.&.A.R.R.
W.&A.

W.&.A.R.R.

W.&.A.R.R.

W.&.A.R.R.

.&.A.R.R.

.R.

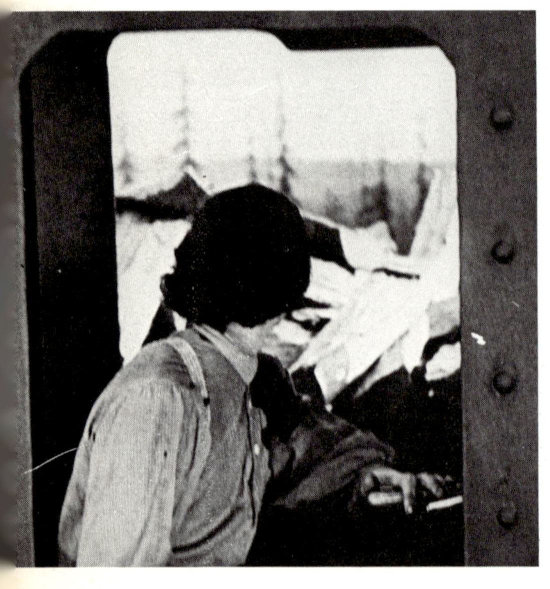

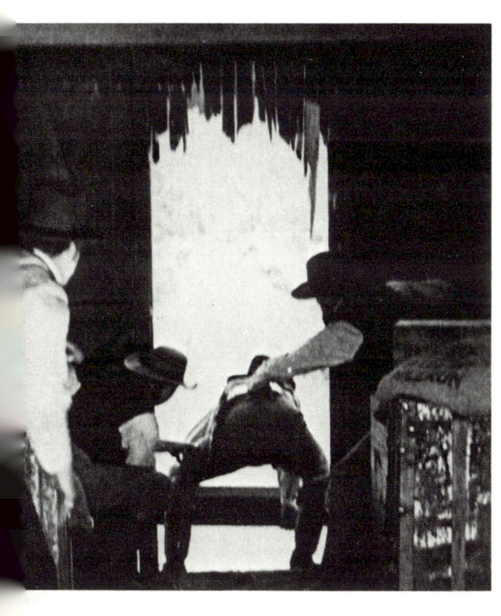

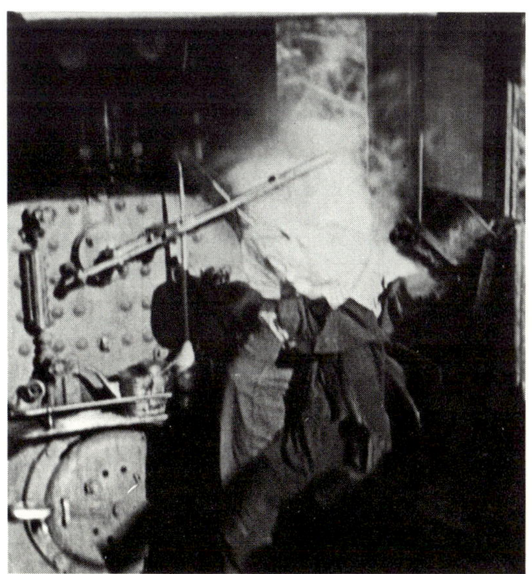

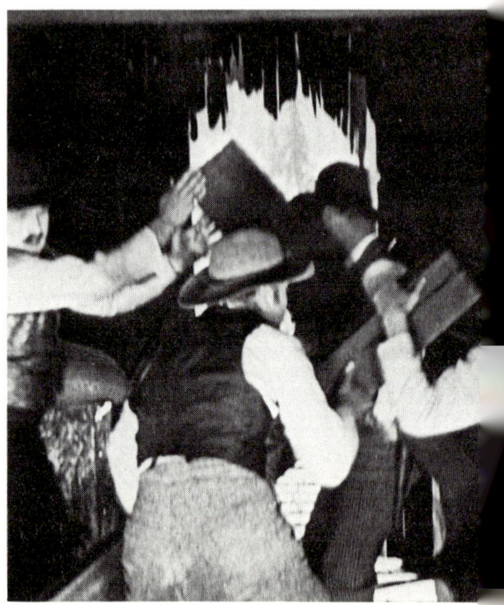

W.8

W.&.A.R.R.

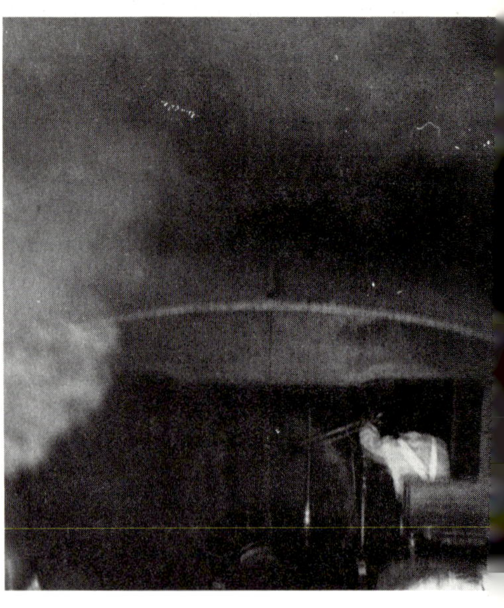

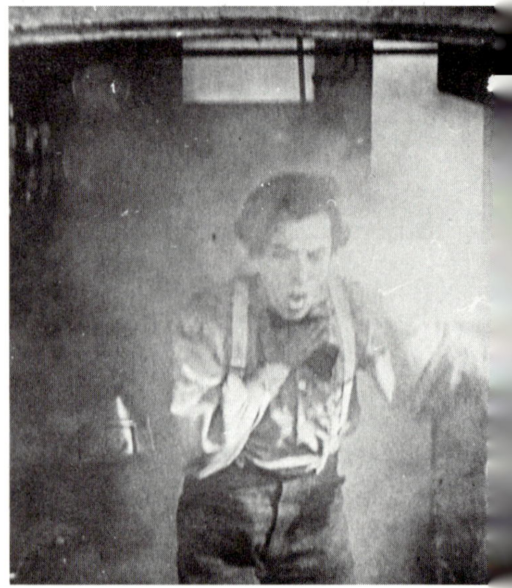

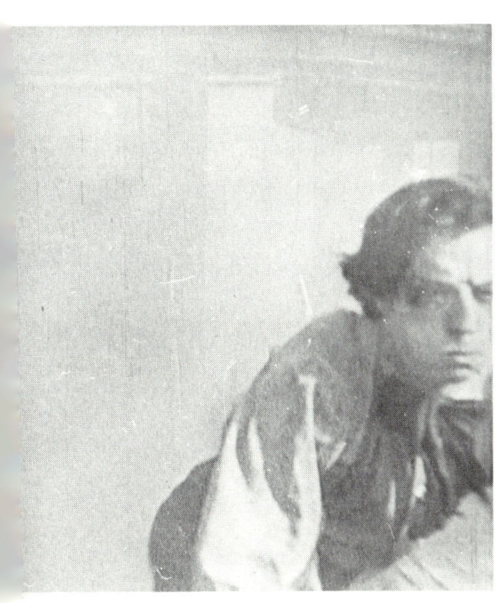

&.A.R.R.

.A.R.R.

.R.R.

.R.R.

.A.R.R.

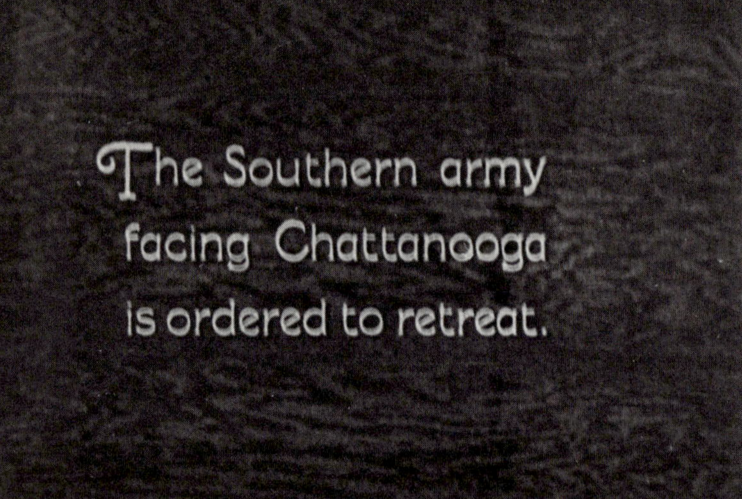
The Southern army
facing Chattanooga
is ordered to retreat.

W.&A.R.R

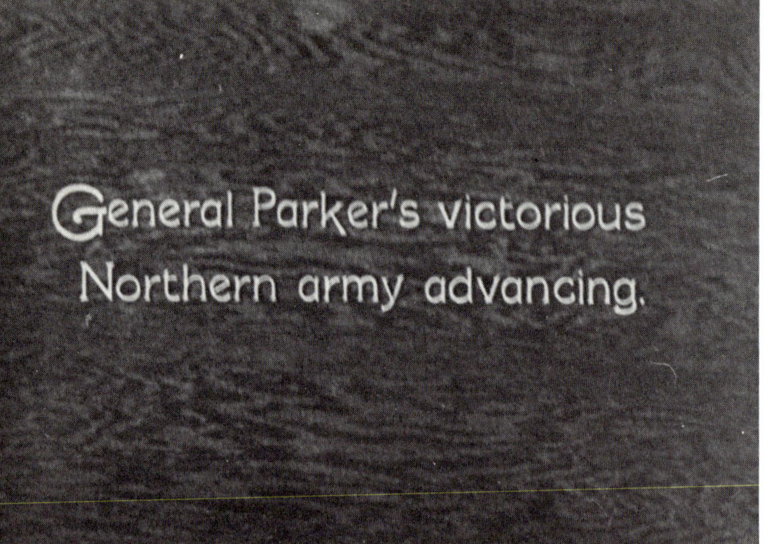

General Parker's victorious
Northern army advancing.

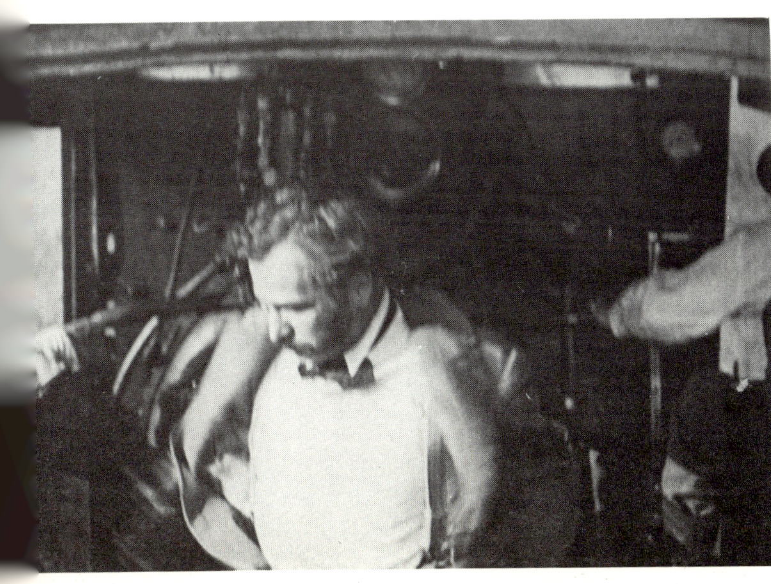 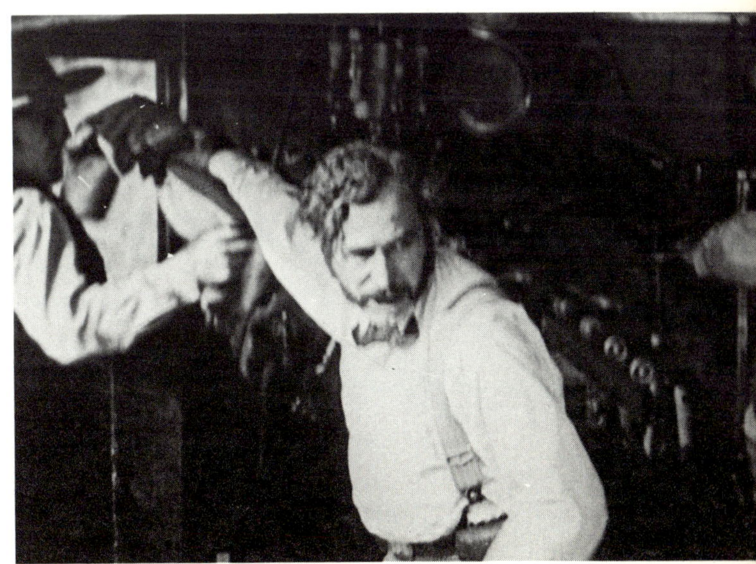

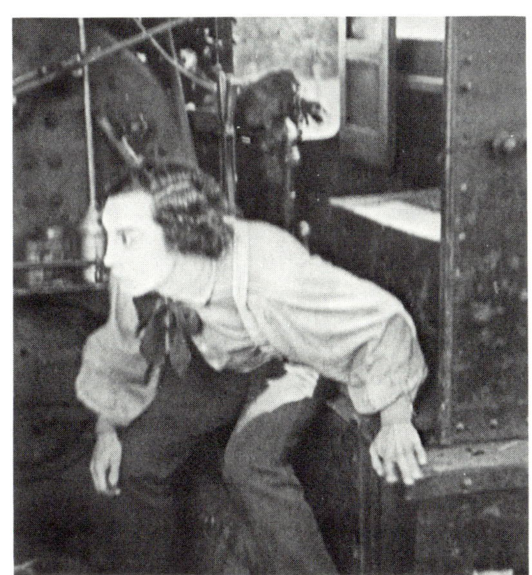

W. & A. R. R.

W. & A. R. R.

B.A.R.R.

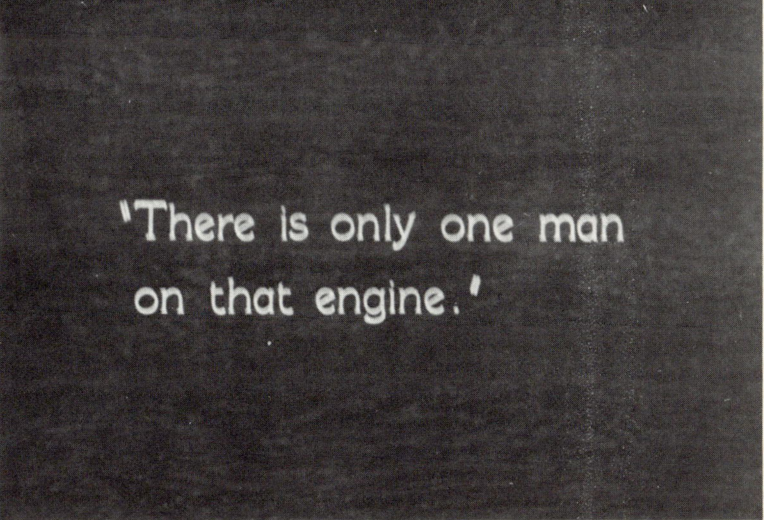
"There is only one man
on that engine."

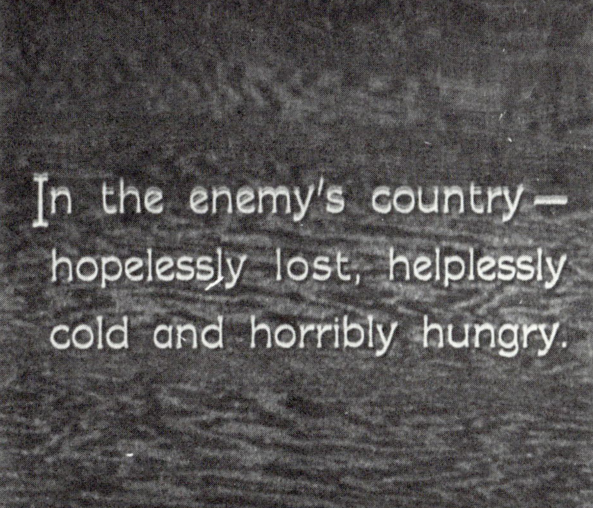
In the enemy's country—
hopelessly lost, helplessly
cold and horribly hungry.
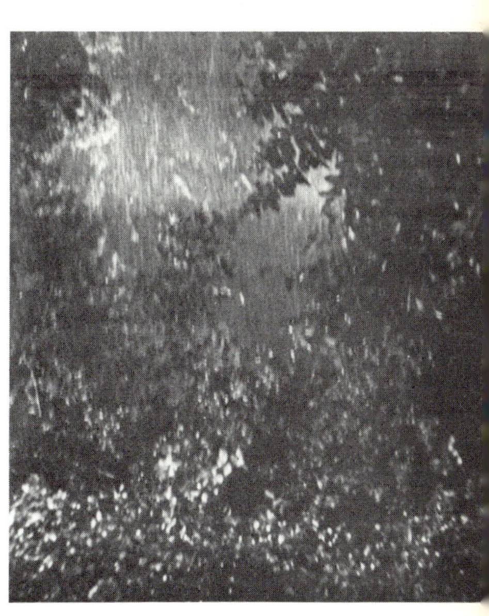

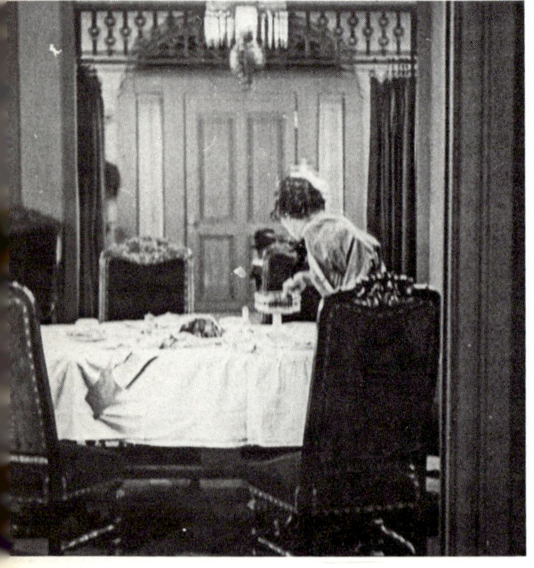

  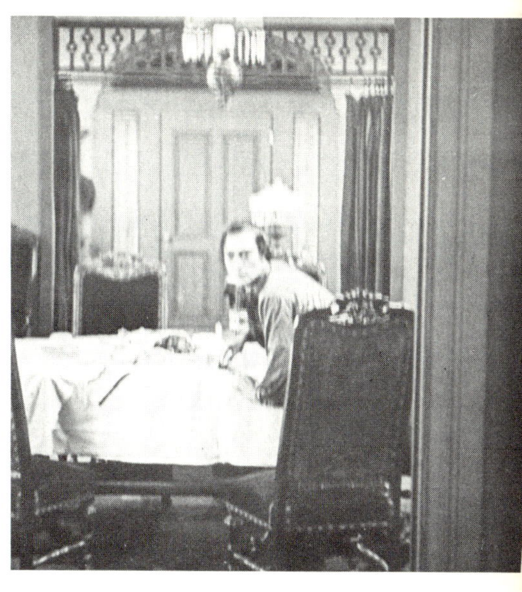

  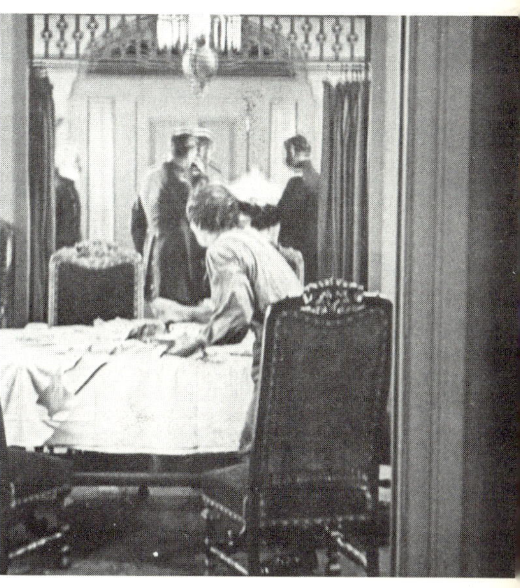

"At nine o'clock tomorrow
morning our supply trains
will meet and unite with
General Parker's army at
the Rock River bridge."

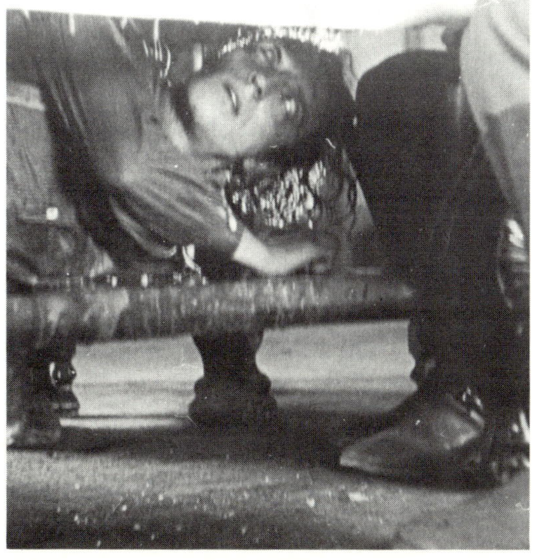

hen the army, backed
our supply trains, will
vance for a surprise
ack on the rebels' left
nk.'

'Once our trains and
troops cross that bridge,
nothing on earth can
stop us.'

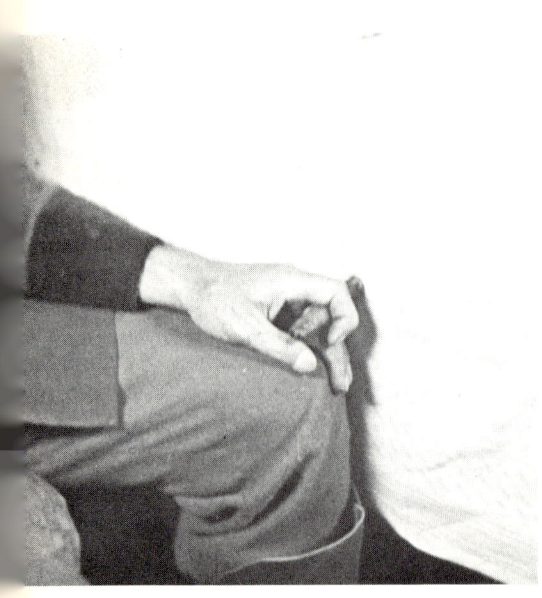

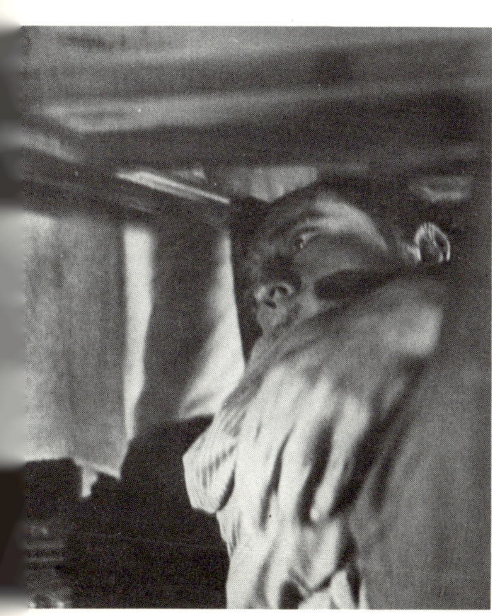

  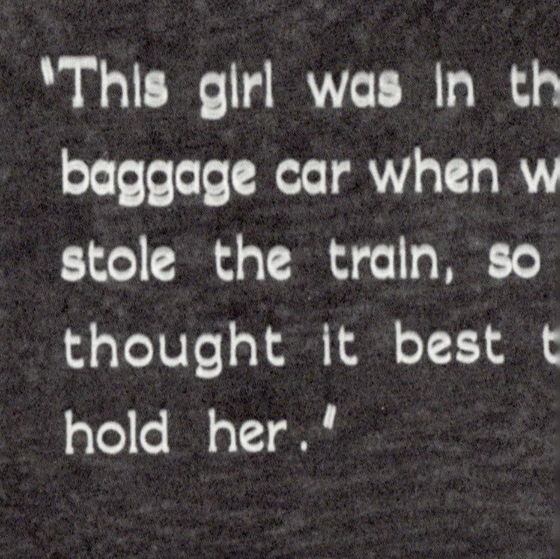
"This girl was in th
baggage car when w
stole the train, so
thought it best t
hold her."

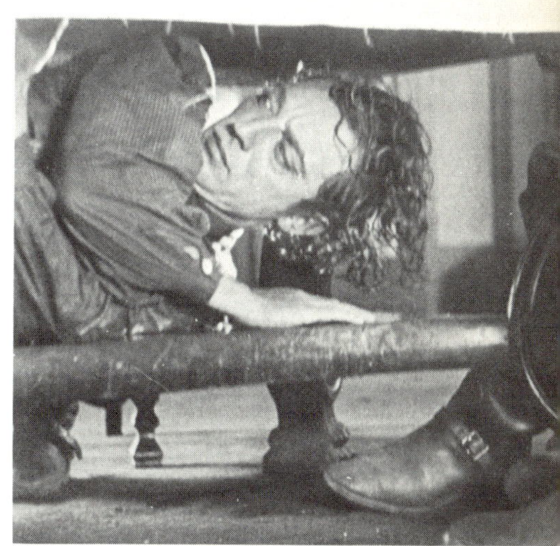

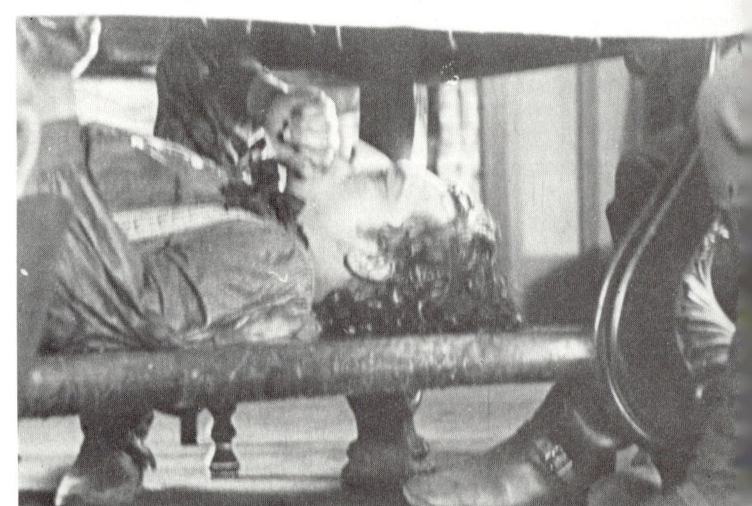

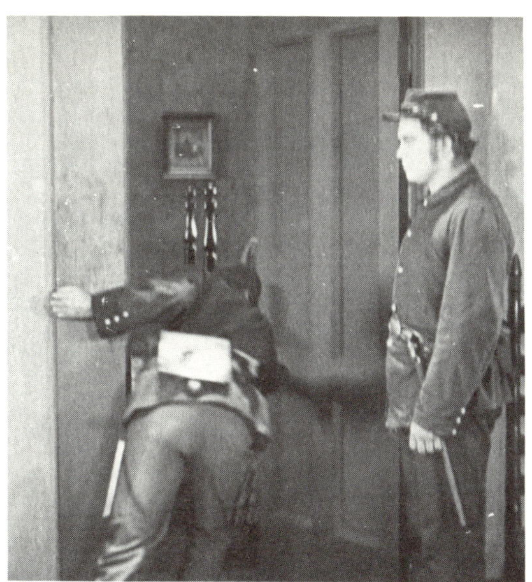

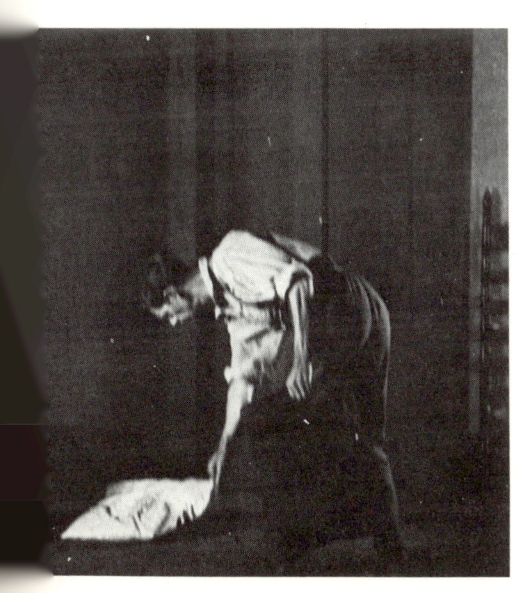

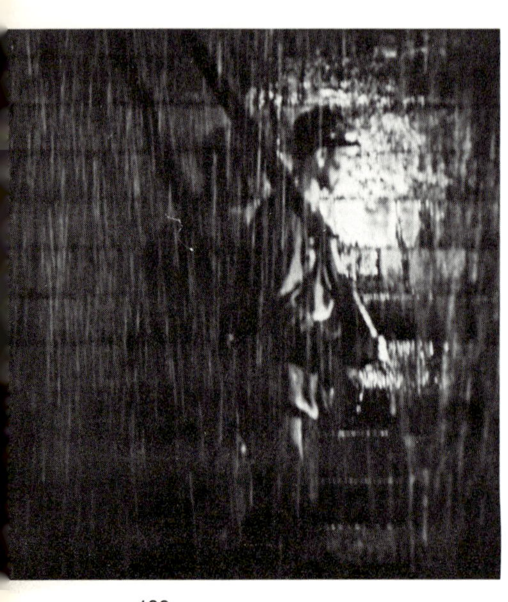

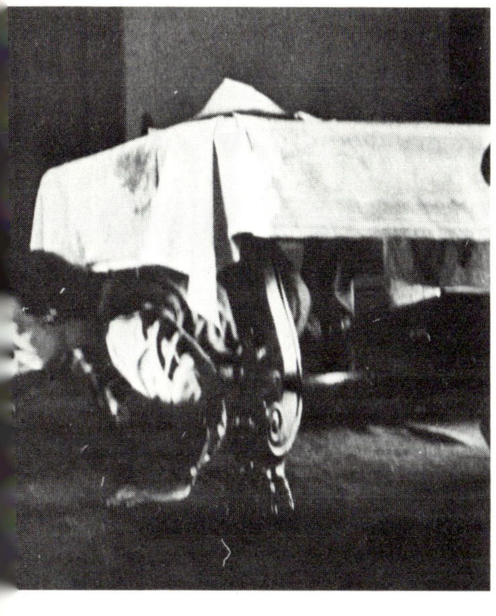

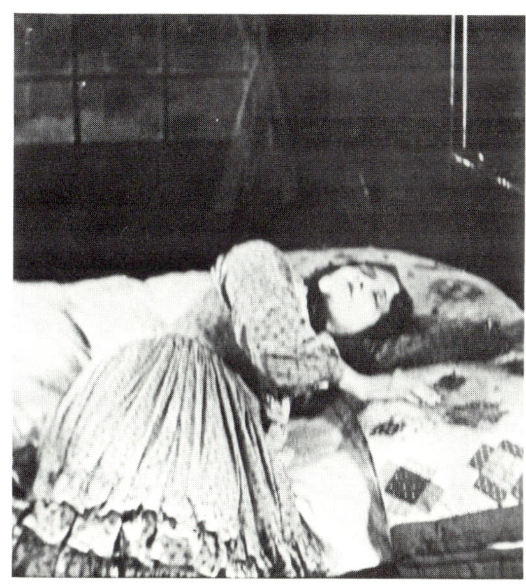

 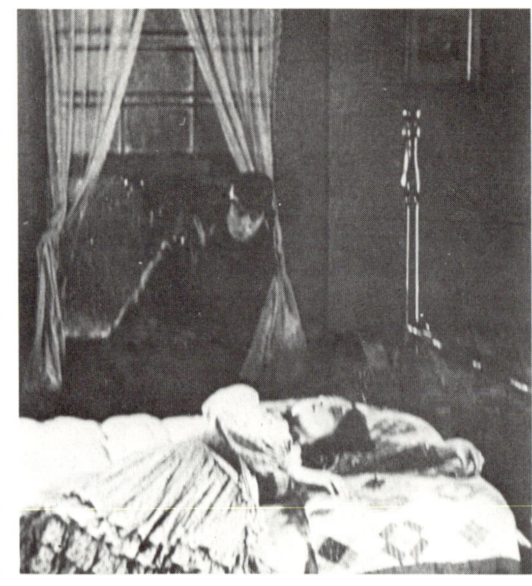 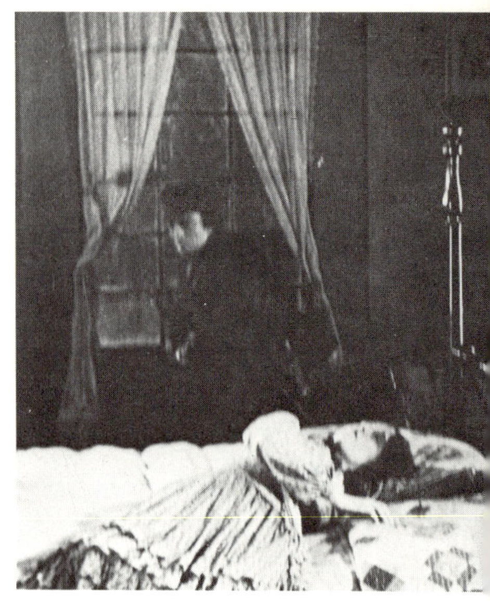

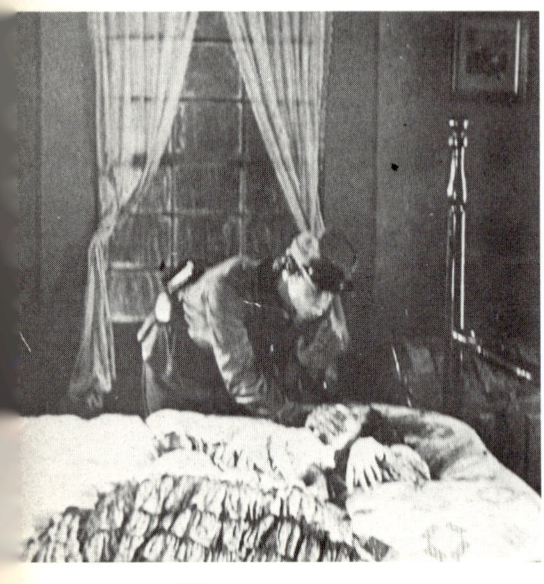 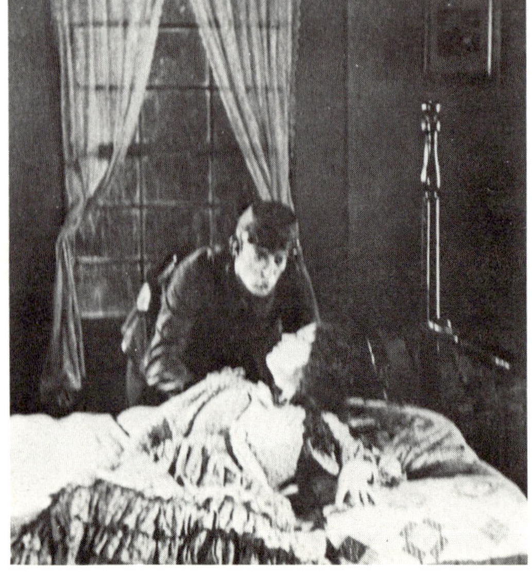 

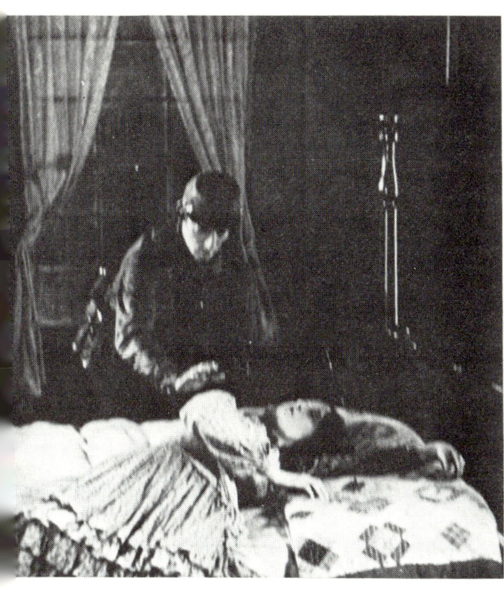
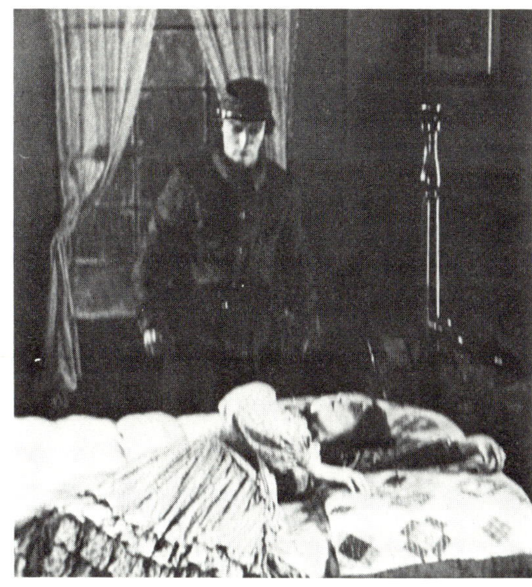

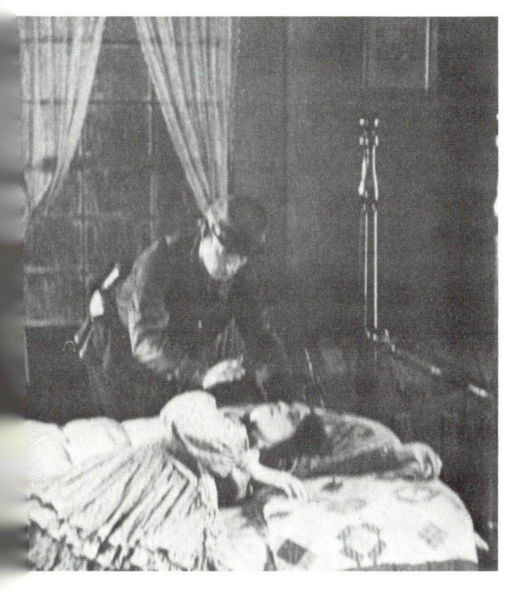
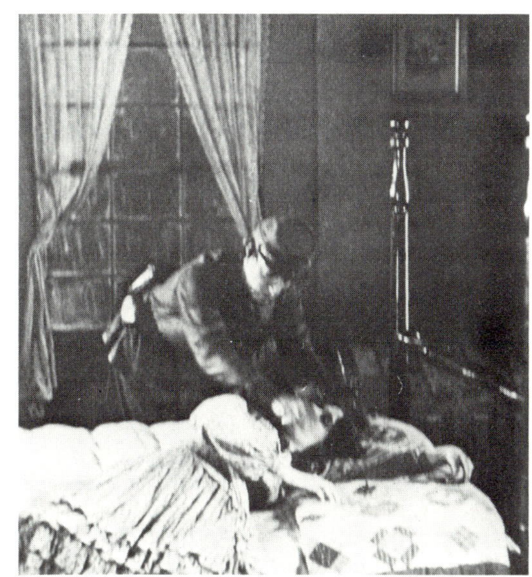
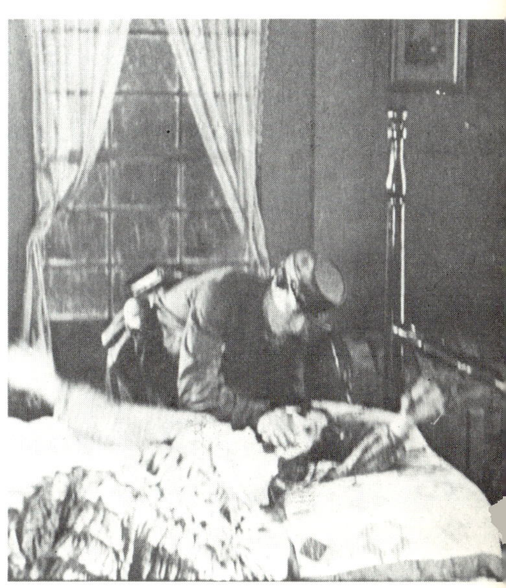

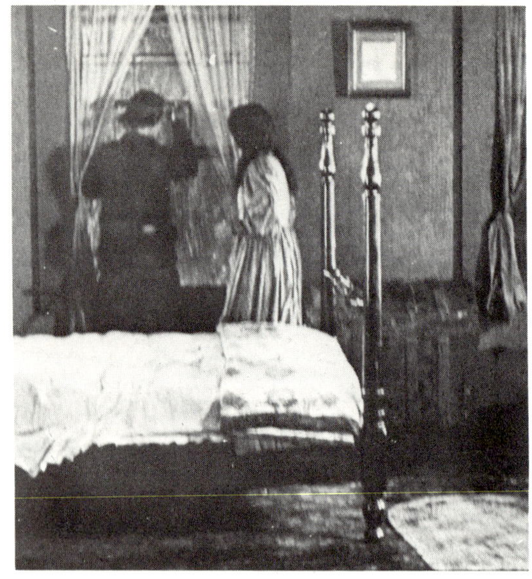
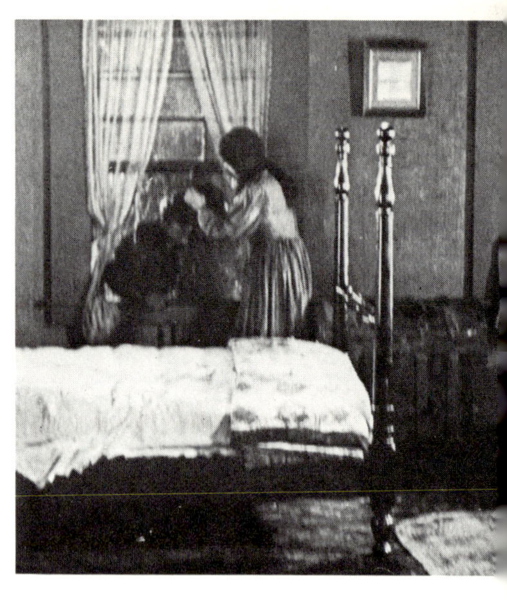
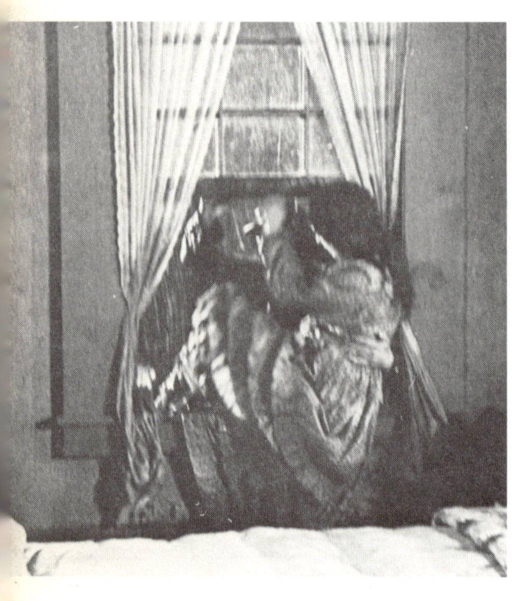

 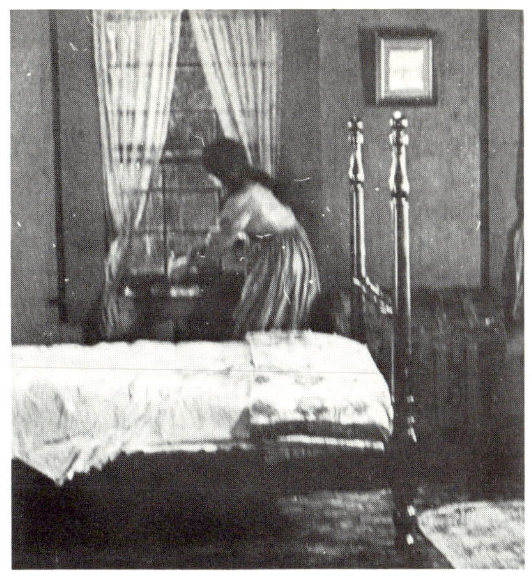 

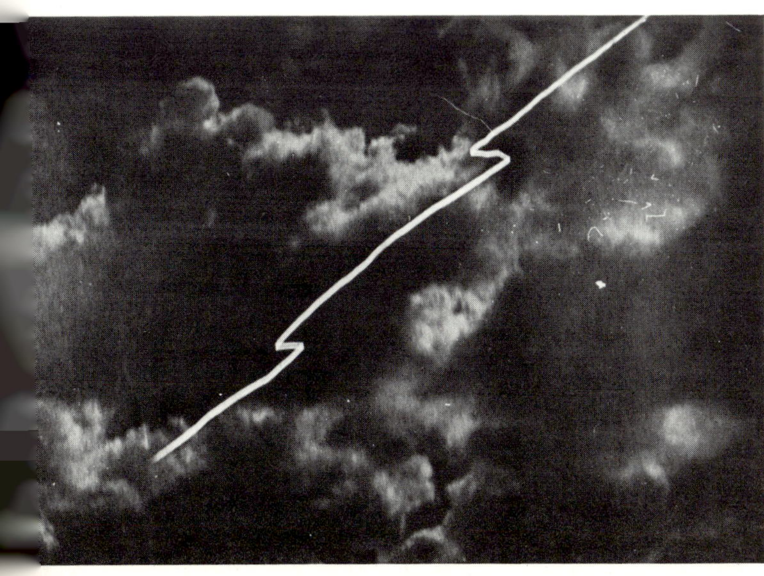 

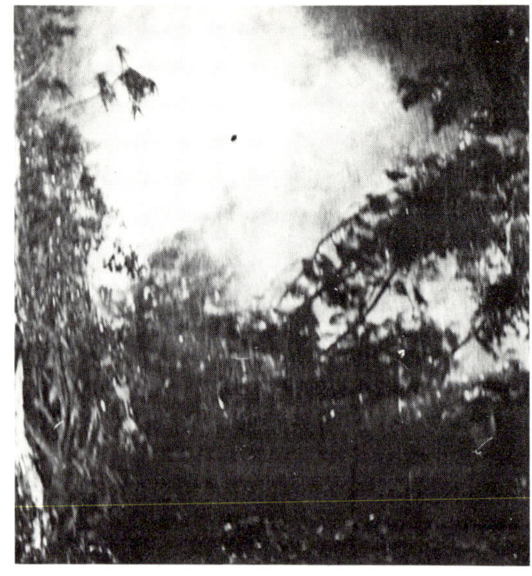

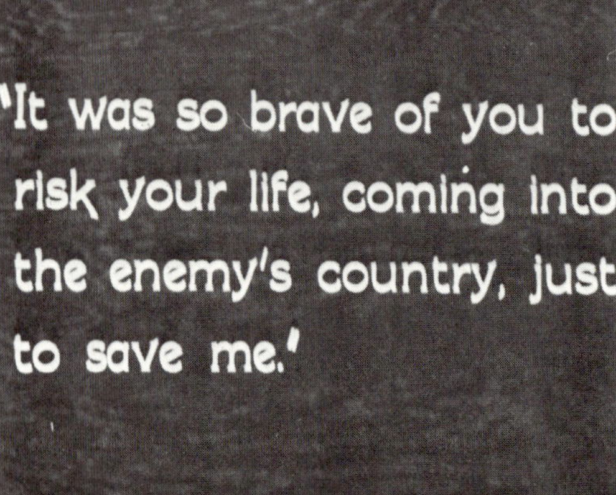
'It was so brave of you to
risk your life, coming into
the enemy's country, just
to save me.'

'We had better stay here
until daybreak to see
where we are.'

After a nice, quiet, refreshing night's rest.

'We've got to get back
to our lines somehow
and warn them of this
coming attack.'

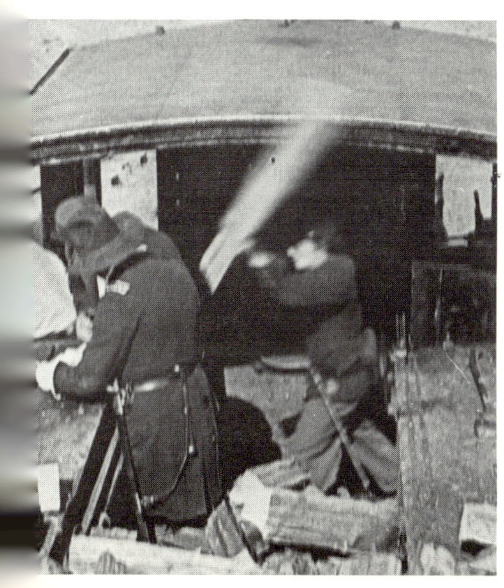

"I will get that spy before he reaches the Southern lines. You follow with the supply trains as planned."

W.&.A.R.R.

U.S.

U.S.M.R.R.

U.S.M.R.R.

W.&A.R.R.

W.B.&A.R.R.

W.B.&A.R.R.

W.B.&A.R.R.

CANADA DRY

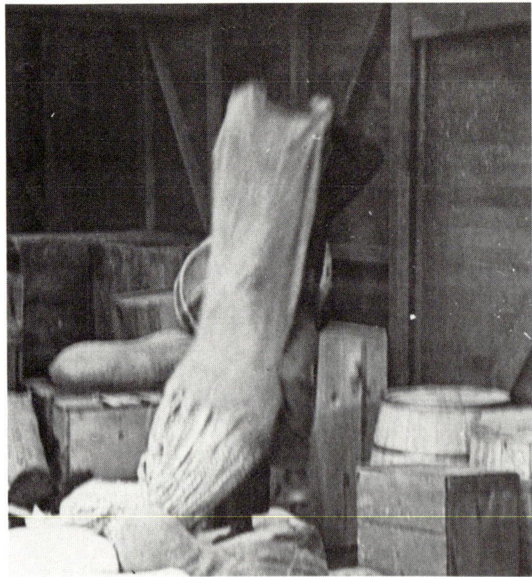

W.&B.A.RR.
TEXAS

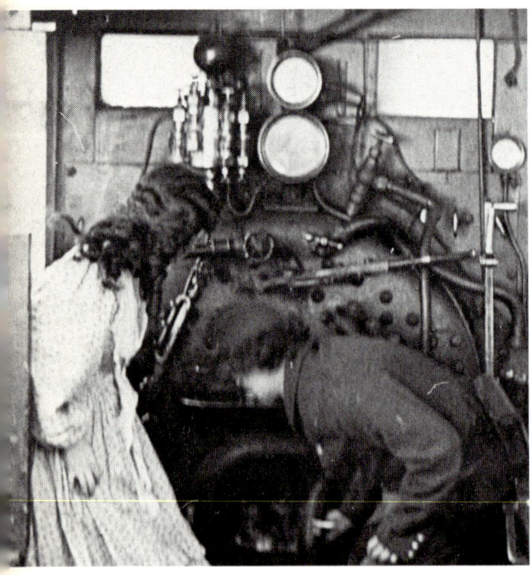

W.&A.R.R.

W.&A.R.R.

W.&A.R.R.

W.&A.R.R.

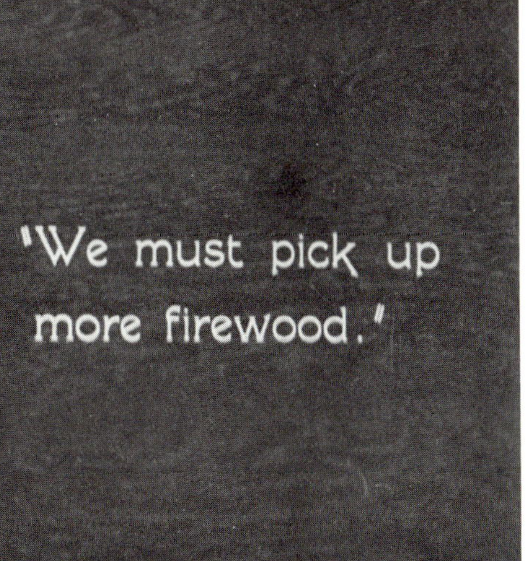

"We must pick up
more firewood."

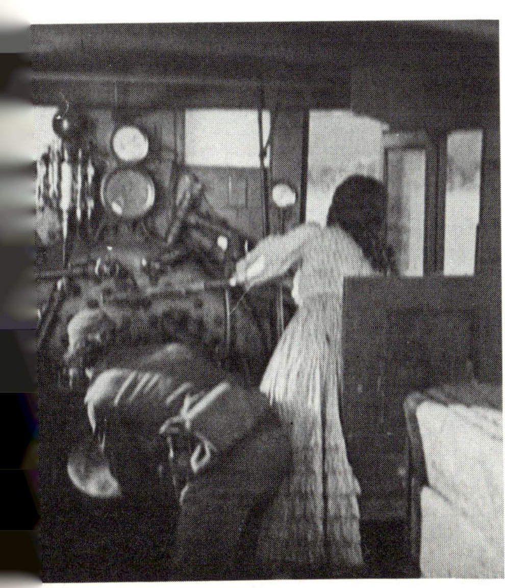  

W.&A.R.R.

W.&A.R.R.

W.&A.

W.&A.R.R.

W.&A.R.R.

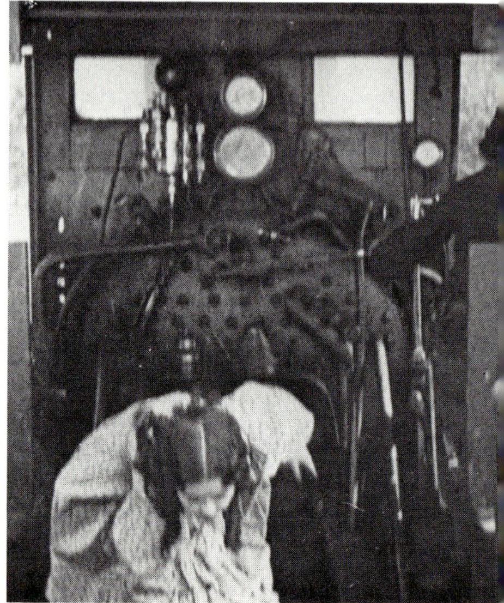

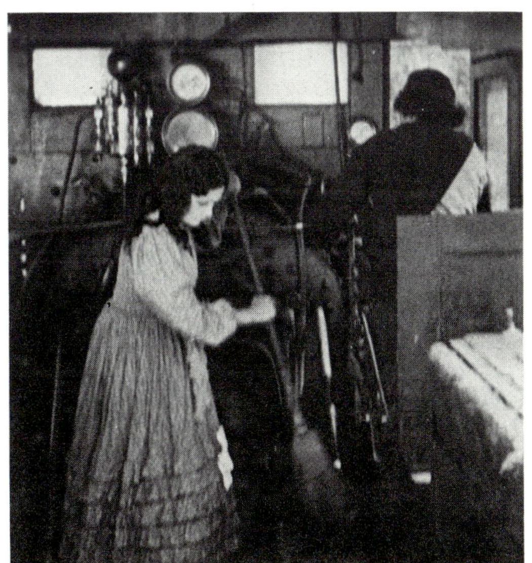

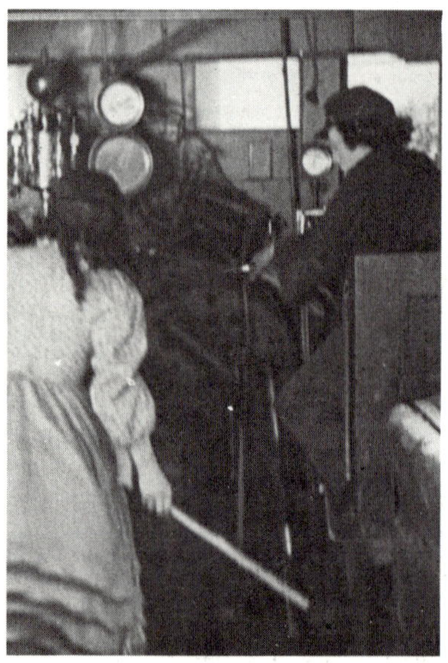

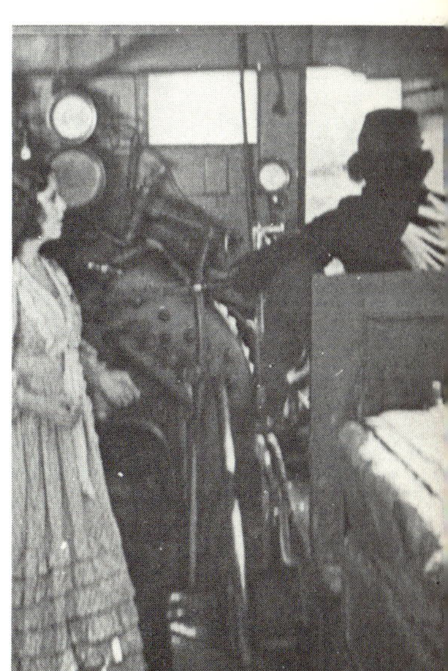

TEXAS
U.S.M.R.R.

U.S.M.R.R.

W.&A.R.R.

W.&A.R.R.

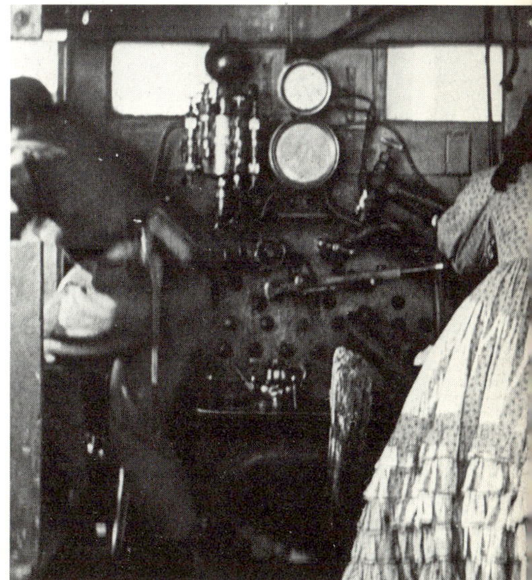

W.&A.R.R.

W.&A.R.R.

The Rock River bridge.

W.&A.R.R.

W.&A.R.R.

W.&A.R.R.

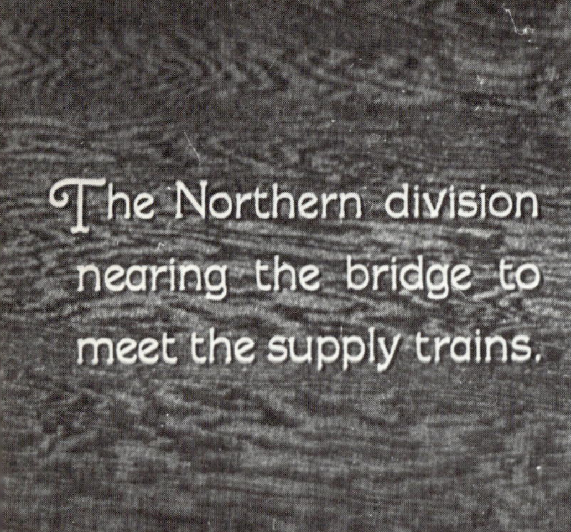
The Northern division
nearing the bridge to
meet the supply trains.

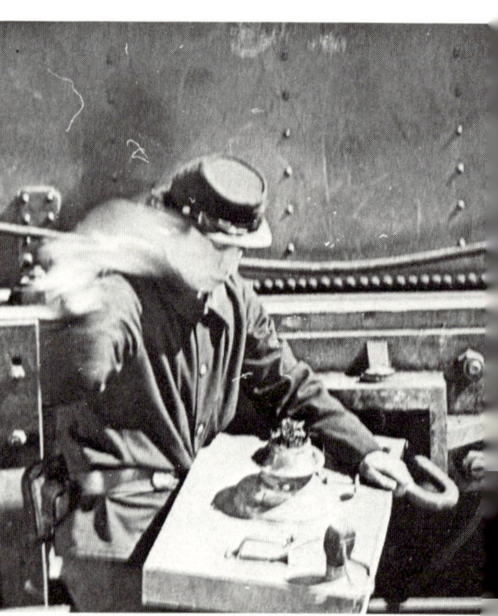

W. & A. R. R.

A. R. R.

R. R.

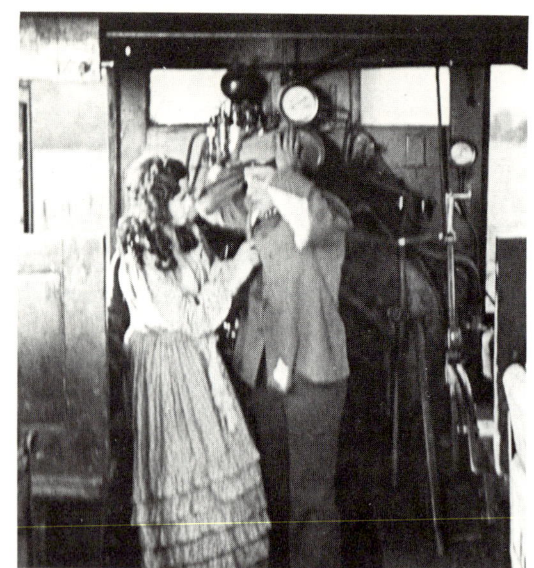

W.&

W.& A.R.R.

DIV. HEADQUARTERS

DIV. HEADQUARTERS

HEADQUARTERS

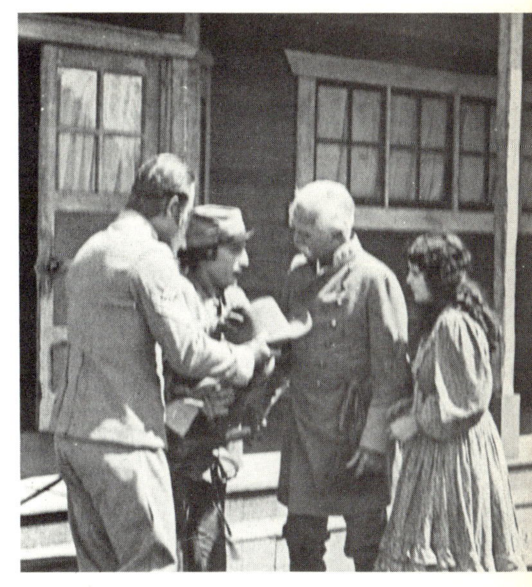

DIV HEADQUARTERS

DIV HEADQUARTERS

DIV HEADQUARTERS

DIV. HEADQUARTERS

'That bridge is not
burned enough to
stop you, and my
men will ford the
river.'

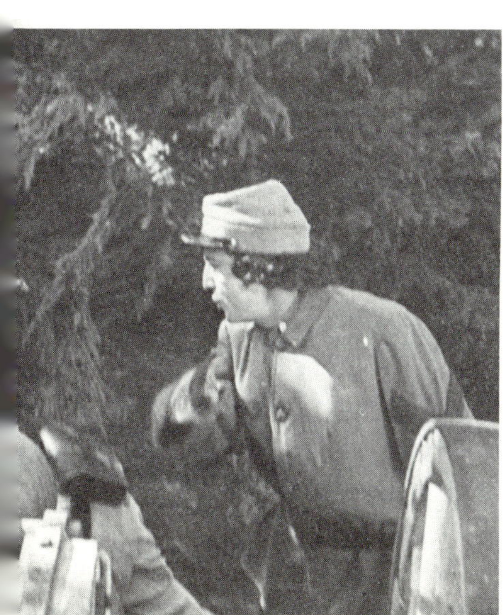

Heroes of the day.

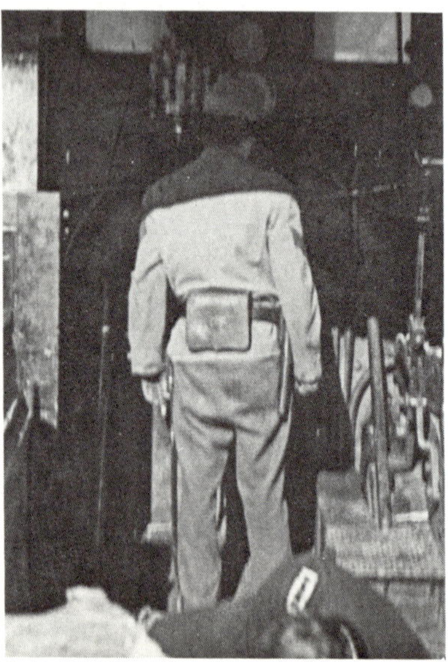

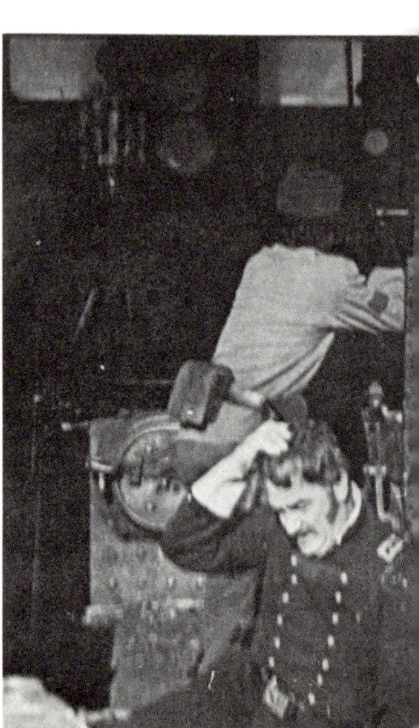

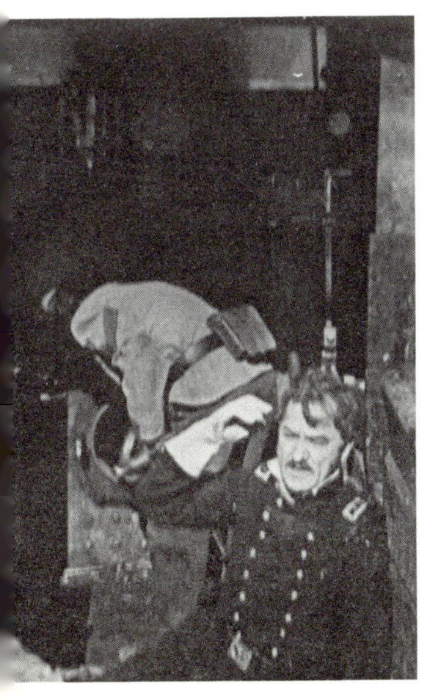
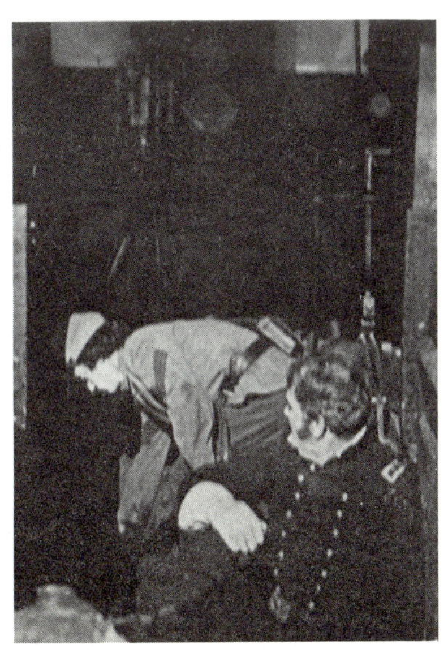

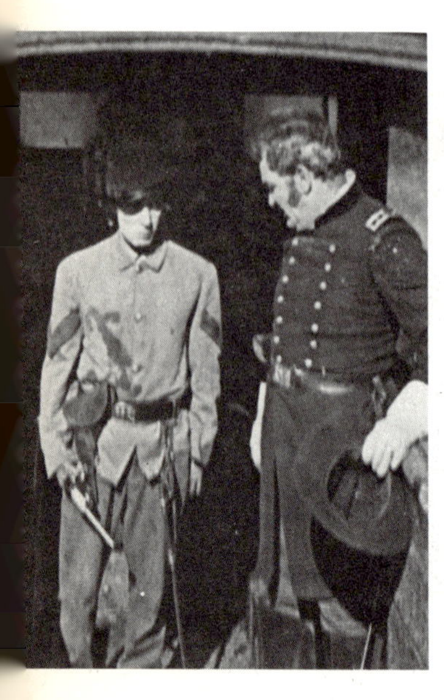

 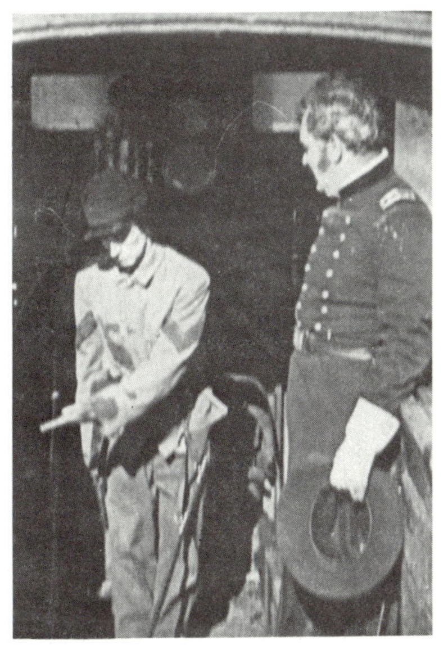  

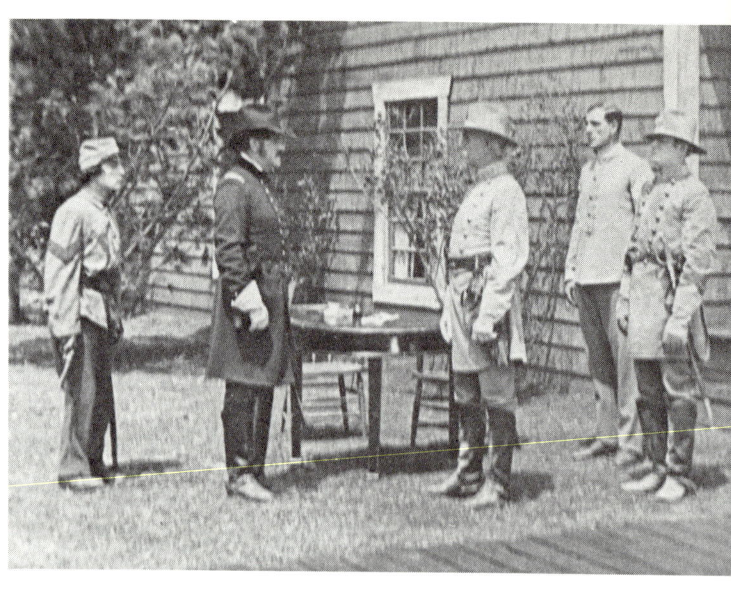

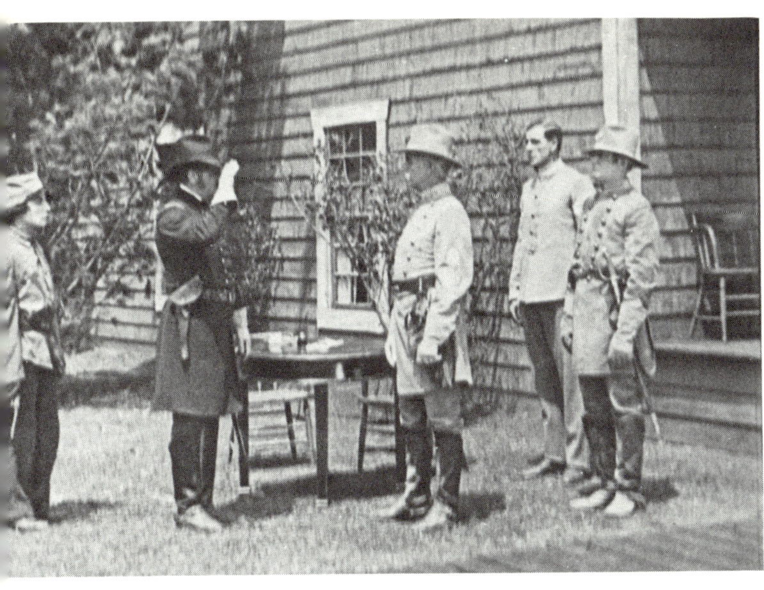 

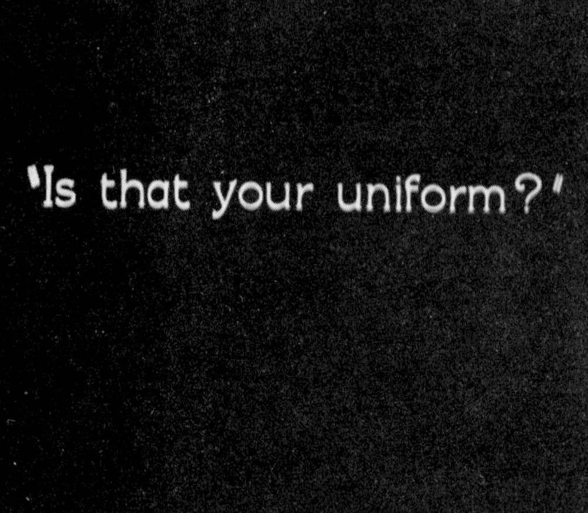
'Is that your uniform?'

'Take it off!'

 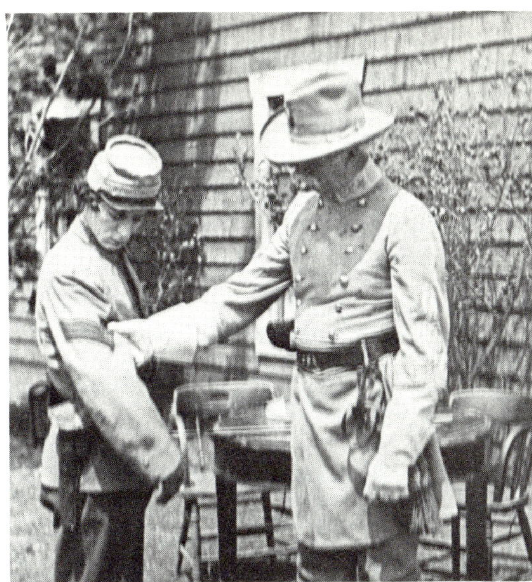 

 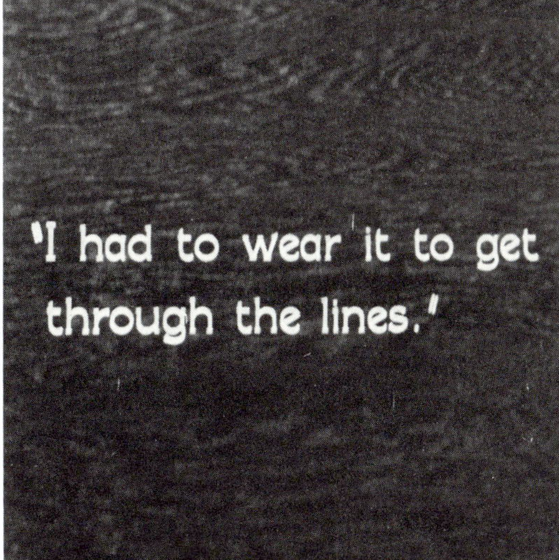

'I had to wear it to get
through the lines.'

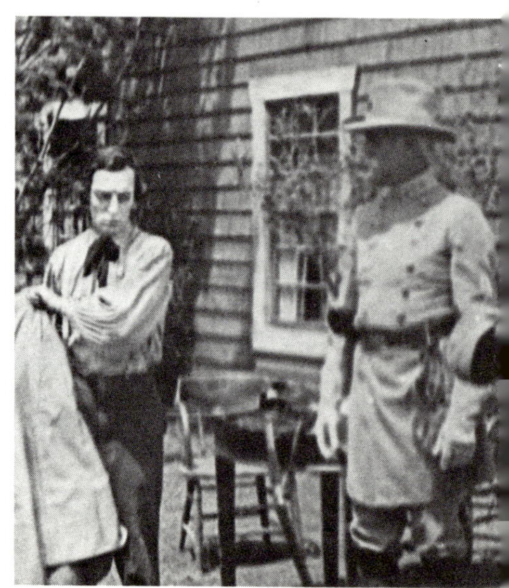

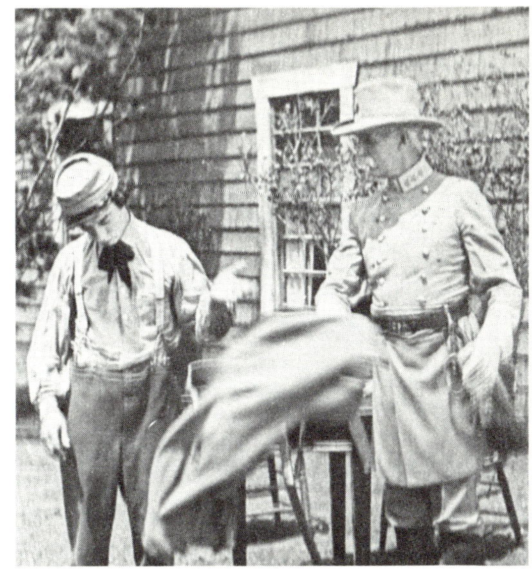

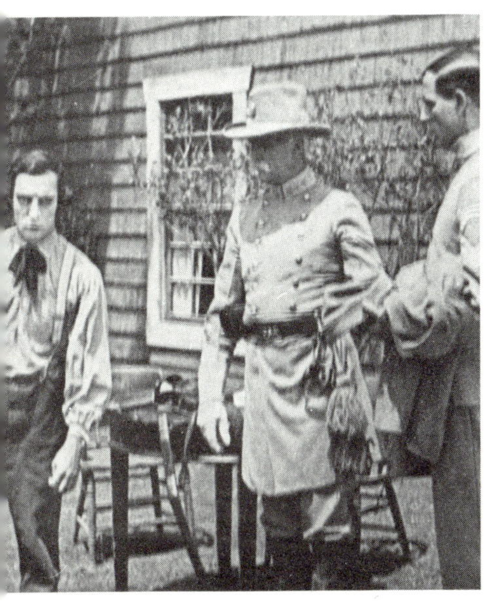

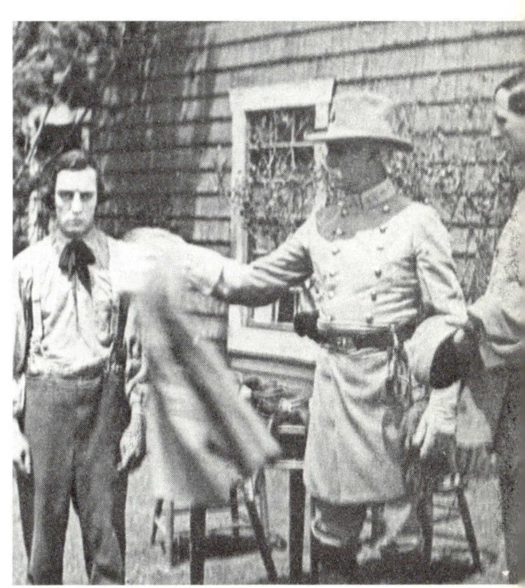

'Enlist the Lieutenant.'

'Occupation?'

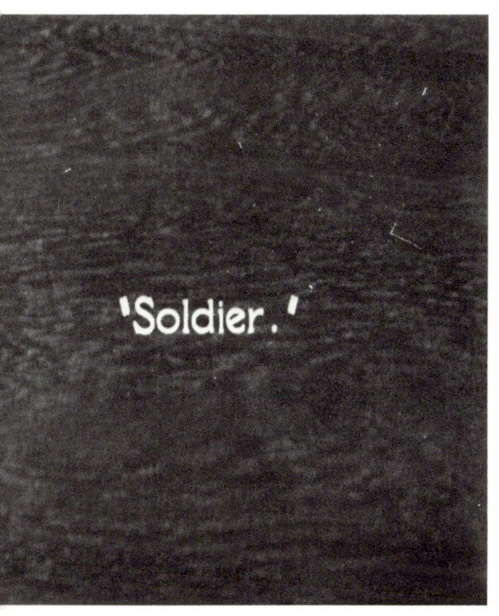
'Soldier.'

THE END